Clio and the Doctors

Jacques Barzun

CLIO AND THE DOCTORS

PSYCHO-HISTORY
QUANTO-HISTORY
& HISTORY

The University of Chicago Press
Chicago and London

The University of Chicago Press, Chicago 60637
The University of Chicago Press, Ltd., London

Printed in the United States of America

International Standard Book Number: 0-226-03849-10 (clothbound)
Library of Congress Catalog Card Number: 74-5723

To My Colleagues
Past and Present
of the Columbia University
History Department
amicitiae causa

CONTENTS

PREFACE

On April 24, 1971, Arthur Schlesinger, Jr., the Schweitzer Professor of History at the City University of New York, held a conference to discuss Psycho-History. The gathering consisted of some thirty historians (academic and other), biographers, sociologists, political scientists, physicians, and psychologists of several schools. About the same time, conferences on the same subject were being held at two other universities in the eastern United States. This heavy concentration of mind on one mode of history paralleled the interest of the general public, which had been aroused by a number of articles and books explaining or exhibiting what was being put forward as a new discipline.

The discussion at the City University, including the three main addresses (one of them mine), was refracted through the medium of the *New York Times* in a long, second-section spread, from which one remark served as the featured Quotation of the Day. Three months later a second *Times* article appeared on the new "tools"—mainly statistical—with which history was being rendered more efficient. These pronouncements, coupled with others proclaiming the death of history or contrasting the advanced procedures with those vaguely called conventional, incited me to write a long essay, which was published in the *American Historical Review* in February 1972. In it I tried to deal with the claims and the results of the new genres, while also defining what I thought History without any prefix was and had always been.

I have now expanded and reorganized the substance of that article, and I have rewritten it with the benefit of criticism from colleagues and readers too numerous to thank individually. My chief aim in making a small book out of a statement has been to lay the issues before the younger generation of students now "taking" history. Their tendency, altogether understandable, is to embrace the new. As in the fine arts, the cult of the new in intellectual matters is now the compulsory, the *conventional* thing, and perhaps it needs to be a little blackened by a devil's advocate, for the same reason that in an earlier generation it was intellectual conservatism which needed to be rebuked and reversed.

Yet on a closer look the actual choice for serious minds is never between an old unsatisfactory mode and a new exciting one. That is mere appearance. The choice is not *between*—it is *among* a multiplicity of tendencies, hopes, pretensions, routines, verbalisms, misrepresentations, fads, discoveries, and genuine new thought. The serious mind, young or old, must by definition work with the true possibilities of the time, not its verbalisms, if anything solid is to come of its efforts.

That is the permanent cultural predicament. The task is to make bricks with the straw supplied to the willing workers. Every age presents its new talents with an enormous amount of fresh stubble, expecting to see it all turned into bricks. These talents go to work and find too late that they were somehow deceived. Hence the possible value of a close inspection of the material now being freely offered to the young historian and the general public.

Let me only add that in my rough analogy, the insubstantial stuff does not stand for any particular works in the new genres; it stands for the assumptions on which they are based, the methods they are said to follow, and the claims that make them so attractive. If the pile of straw on the opposite side of the argument is of tougher fiber, it is because critics have used their pitchforks on it for a longer time.

Introduction: Who Are the Doctors?

Innovation in Historiography

The notion that to possess interest and value a man, an idea, or an object should be "of its own time" is an historical notion which, if true, is just as applicable to history itself as to any other subject.* The only question is how to judge what is of its own time: survivals and anachronisms are so plentiful. This difficulty is usually settled by finding out whether something that is new and thriving in a separate but possibly relevant field is being neglected, not taken advantage of. Thus when the zipper has been perfected, a garment capable of harboring one yet lacking it is felt to be primitive and unsatisfactory.

In other words, the example of technology has influenced our judgments universally. We want the latest device because we think it can best fulfill our needs. In the scientific study of nature there is a continual headlong rush to use as soon as possible whatever new resources of thought and equipment the market affords. The same thing has happened, is happening to the study of history. In the classic statement of the need,

*In these pages the word *history* stands for the written report, not the actuality, of the past. History-as-event is termed *the past, past events,* etc. This distinction is not, of course, maintained in passages quoted from other authors, nor in common expressions such as "philosophy of history" or "the lesson of history," or "history was made when the two great powers signed, etc." It is hoped that no ambiguity will result from the very occasional use of such ready-made phrases.

and the answer to the need, given by Professor William L. Langer in 1958, this idea of improvement by technical means elsewhere available is explicit. The historians assembled to hear from their president about "The Next Assignment" were first told that they lacked "the 'speculative audacity' of the natural scientists" and tended to be "buried in their own conservatism." History had indeed expanded its horizons beyond political history, but there is "still ample scope for penetration in depth. . . . I refer more specifically to the urgently needed deepening of our historical understanding through exploitation of the concepts and findings of modern psychology."[1]

But the doctor of psychology is only one of the physicians now preoccupied with the state of the patient, History. The others have been trained in sociology, anthropology, and demography, and are equipped with the technique of numbers appropriate to those subjects, which is statistics. Following their example, historians are turning into statisticians, having "come to appreciate the effectiveness of statistical tools in coping with the problem of finding uniformities . . . and . . . providing the means of making inductive inferences by logically defensible procedures. . . . A number of members of the profession have come to hope that a variety of different kinds of historical problems, heretofore discussed only in rather general terms, can by such means be treated more effectively and brought closer to a solution on the basis of ordered knowledge."[2]

The rebuke is polite but clear and it shows in what respects History is thought to be ailing. Just as Professor Langer by requiring *deeper* knowledge implied present shallowness, so the statisticians imply that historiography now lacks *ordered* knowledge and defensible procedures. With these defects remedied, it could solve problems. The verdict, then, is superficiality, intellectual irresponsibility, and futility. Treatment is called for and this the psycho-historian and the quanto-historian will provide.

But failure is not all that is adduced to show the present plight of History. Empirical observation also suggests that History is sick, dying, dead. Whether one looks at the numbers enrolled in history courses or the tendency of history departments to make sheep's eyes at bold quantifiers, or the declining popularity of history among general readers (they gorge on lush biographies instead), it is clear that the nineteenth-century pre-eminence of history in the sphere of intellect no longer obtains. The historical sense in modern populations is feeble or nonexistent, as Ortega pointed out, even though the mania for keeping records, building archives, and celebrating trivial anniversaries is rampant. Indeed it is probably the decline of a true sense of history that encourages those pseudo-historical manifestations.

In any event, the combination of the dominant social sciences ("social studies" in the lower schools), the cult of the new in art, commerce, technology, and natural science, and the numerous anxieties expressing themselves in "futurism" (planning, forecasting, "educating for the year 2000," and other forms of astrology) has created the impression that History can no longer speak in an important way to the contemporary world.

The historical cast of common thought remains, but it has apparently become too banal to be trusted. Without any sense of contradiction, the student who is drawn to the study of history in college or graduate school wonders what secrets his instructor can teach him. He asks what the methods are, the ingenious indirect means comparable to those of physical and social science, that he can set out to master. He asks and wonders in vain. There is nothing arcane and elaborate, it seems, that he can go and be industrious about, and thus prove himself a proficient while assuaging his intellectual insecurity—nothing, except the old familiar search for documents and the play of imagination and judgment upon them.

For some, moreover, the indeterminacy of history is still more unsettling. They want to see all past events coming out of some namable source. They obviously do not come out of anybody's sack of notes, for that is only the work of finite mind upon relics supplied more or less accidentally. There must be something solid underlying all and making all intelligible, barring a few unruly particulars. The example of Marx is there to show how a narrow glance, if properly directed, can take in the whole world; whereas the contrary attitudes all leave history to its natural confusion, unexplained. As confusion, history might continue to be a pastime; it might survive as a lesser branch of literature, but it could no longer serve living purposes. It must be transformed by new methods into explanations, preferably quantified, of the great social problems of the day. The records of the past must be made to answer questions about the cause of war, the roots of inequality, the psychology of power, the buried motives of persecution.

The Urge to Merge: Earlier Demands

The invitation or admonition addressed to historians in the light of these requirements and possibilities is not new. When scholars native and foreign were celebrating the centenary of the Louisiana Purchase at St. Louis in 1904, the historians listened to the great Karl Lamprecht, who came from Leipzig to tell them that "history is primarily a psycho-sociological science. . . . The new progressive and therefore aggressive point of view . . . is the socio-psychological, which may be termed modern. . . . The rise of sociology and anthropology during the last decades . . . has meant a fresh start in the writing of cultural history and in the development of method. . . . It is only the beginning of an intensive psycho-sociological method."[3]

In the rest of his remarks, Lamprecht argues that the writing of political history is out of date and that the traditional attention given to leading figures is a falsification of historical truth. What he advocates reflects the radical reconstruction of the social sciences that culminated in the 1890s: anthropology, sociology, psychology, and statistical method were made over new. In comparison with them, history looked old and worn, shallow and inexact. It had been a delusion to suppose with Ranke and his school that history had become scientific: it had merely become blindly exhaustive about past politics.* It produced what was wittily called "biennial history"—a lifetime of research to furnish an account of two years in a bygone era, preferably remote. An injection of youthful intelligence was needed to revive History, and its secret was "methods."

In other words, the debate on the "plight" and the "death" of History was the same seventy years ago as today, and the forecasts and remedies also: the only History worth having would make use of the progressive ologies—chiefly psychology and sociology. It would acknowledge the importance of the mass of men and their collective life by discarding the great-man theory of historical propulsion. Faced with these masses, the historian must address himself to social ques-

*"If there is one thing which, more than another, is the mark of Oxford today, it is belief in contemporary documents, exact testing of authorities, scrupulous verification of citations, minute attention to chronology, geography, paleography, and inscriptions. When all these are right, you cannot go wrong" (Frederic Harrison, "The History Schools," in *The Meaning of History* [New York and London, 1902 (orig. 1893)], pp. 118–38).

tions, in the study of which he must count and measure. As individuals, men would then be *understood* by the advanced psychology; acting together as nations, classes, or other groups, they would be *explained* by the new quantitative sociology and its laws.*

From the repetition today of those exhortations dating from early in our century (and which even then gave rise to a *Methodenstreit*), we might infer that the first burst of doctrine brought no results. And yet the interval was not lacking in accomplishments. Social history established itself as an historical specialty; the so-called new history gave primacy to the force of ideas in the stream of events, replacing as it were great men by great books; and psychological technicalities served the interpreter of character in biography, where they still exert undisputed sway.

The question, "Yes, but *what* psychology?" is important, and the answer given affects the judgment that one is led to pass upon the psycho-histories of our time. As to this answer, Professor Langer had no doubts when he gave out his "next assignment": "I do not refer to classical or academic psychology which, so far as I can detect, has little bearing on historical problems, but rather to psychoanalysis and its later developments and variations as included in the terms 'dynamic' or 'depth psychology.' "[4] A query of the same kind must obviously be addressed to all the other social sciences offering themselves in marriage to History—which anthropology? whose sociology? and it poses a difficulty of a peculiarly historical sort: How

*Besides the social sciences mentioned by Lamprecht, there also flourished at the turn of the century an Anthroposociology particularly associated with the name of Leon Gumplowicz. It was the latest avatar of racial anthropology, and as such it carried forward the never-ending search for a human typology. See J. Barzun, *Race, a Study in Superstition*, rev. ed. (New York, 1965), pp. 158 ff.

does the historian choose from whom to learn and to borrow among the schools of behavioral science and among their evolving phases? If Lamprecht, with his eye on the new sciences of 1904, was right in theory, should practice have waited until psychoanalysis and game theory had established themselves fifty years later? What one concludes affects Method and Substance, as we shall shortly find.

Meanwhile, a brief look at the "new" biography of the earlier twentieth century will serve to bring out recurring features of the "new methods" advocacy. To take biography is convenient, despite the differences between biography and history, because psychology in its accepted meaning is the study of the mind; its utility to the historian is therefore most obvious when he is dealing with one individual, when he is a biographer.

As early as 1913, Preserved Smith attempted a psychoanalytic study of Luther—"a highly neurotic personality"—but his essay had no sequel and apparently no imitators.[5] Yet one can now see that it was a foreshadowing of the movement of ideas which came into prominence in the 1920s and 30s: the belated recognition of Freud, the general discovery of anthropology as a way of looking at contemporary society, the growing habit of psychologizing.* The New Biography was a faithful embodiment of these influences. It achieved popularity because it professed to be for the first time truly psychological, indeed clinical. It established a new vocabulary and a new attitude. It was concerned with "depth" (that is, the hidden and un-

*Psychologizing may be defined as the practice of taking an utterance or an action not at its face value as an expression of straightforward desire or purpose, but as an involuntary symptom which, when properly interpreted, discloses a meaning hidden from the agent and from common observers. It is a form of the genetic fallacy (see below p. 65).

conscious) and with "science" as the instrument of disclosure. The new genre was the occasion of much theorizing;[6] its materials, not to say its victims, could not of course be the great figures dismissed as unimportant by Lamprecht and others at the turn of the century: the new biographies were about the same figures no longer great.

What *History without Psychology and Sociology?*

These tendencies in biography were the enriched expression of an old naturalism. Although in the twenties Lytton Strachey was looked upon as the inspired inventor of the new genre—the genius who could in a few pages distill character out of indigestible masses of fact—he himself acknowledged that he had behind him the example of Sainte-Beuve, each of whose *Lundis* was a portrait drawn by a "naturalist of souls." And had Strachey inquired, he could have found in an American, Gamaliel Bradford, a precursor who as early as 1895 produced a collection of what he would soon call "psychographs" under the title *Types of American Character.* According to Bradford, the graph was dictated by Nature herself[7]—and she went on dictating at a great rate to fill out Bradford's numerous and well-received volumes over a span of forty years.

In the eyes of a generation equipped with computers and adept at real, not metaphorical, graphs, all the foregoing is bound to look amateurish; but the topic under discussion is theory, and in theory those primitive performances expressed as fully as ours the resolve to interpret, first biography, then history, by modern methods. Strachey's *Elizabeth and Essex,* Bradford's collected works, and innumerable other books are moldering on the shelves to prove it.

Indeed, well before Bradford, the study of types numbered many practitioners, in social science and elsewhere. Balzac thought of his vast novel in a hundred volumes as a "zoology" in which social types took the place of animal species.[8] All the physical anthropologists of the nineteenth century were adept at drawing character sketches on the basis of the facial angle and at inferring social status and political opinions from the measurement of skulls. In short, the impulse to correlate mental traits with graveyard relics or other historical data is part and parcel of the historical search itself.

The memory of how men have *in fact* written about their past should therefore moderate the claims of the new behavioral sciences. Since History recounts the doings of men it cannot take ten steps without describing character, mores, and social arrangements. Earliest of chroniclers in the West, Homer tells us that Nestor was wise, Ulysses wily, and Thersites ugly, deformed, unhappy, and hence a malicious agitator against authority—the first physio-psycho-sociology of dissent. The histories (properly, the researches) of Herodotus also analyze motive and contain an anthropology and a sociology of the regions he visited. Next, Aristotle writes like a sociologist-historian when he tries to find the causes of revolutions and gives, in a chapter that has not yet been improved on, the logical and psychological sequence of the forms of government. Plutarch, the earliest professional biographer in our tradition, uses symptomatic anecdotes to delineate character—"a light occasion, a word, or some sport"—because they make "men's dispositions more plain than famous battles won." But he also fills his comparisons of paired Greeks and Romans with general principles, as if hoping to come upon the laws of human action by assembling common features out of different circumstances. Autobiographers, whether the pagan Marcus Aurelius or the Christian Saint Augustine, were obviously attracted to their subjects by the desire to analyze interesting characters. (Augustine is particularly good about libido in babies and the earliest signs of infant rivalry.) Tacitus is chock-full of character analyses with which he explains events; and for sheer relentlessness, the "Secret History" of Procopius could give points to any later example of interpretation based on the lower depths of human passion.

The Issue to Be Settled

In short, psycho-history and its congeners form the latest wave in a succession of waves that began with the writing of history itself. To be sure, the object of curiosity varies. After the anthropological interest satisfied by Herodotus comes the political preoccupation of Thucydides, who criticizes his predecessor. With each historian or school the change marks a redirection of attention, not advance or improvement. The pendulum swings. The narrow view begets the desire for breadth, after which the need is felt again for close scrutiny. The shift from one outlook to the other no doubt corresponds to timely needs, and for that reason it strikes the contemporaries as a step toward perfection; but it is not progress. After two or three alternations, the new phase might just as appropriately be called reactionary as progressive.

It is idle, therefore, to allege "resistance to progress" when one demurs from the latest claim that "at last" history is going to be made whole by the adjunction of the science of mind or the science of society. The point to settle is what the new discipline purposes to do, and how. Again and again, the object has been to overcome the uncertainty and superficiality of history, to reach and reason out the supposed mechanism under the moving platform upon which mankind enacts its destiny. That is the goal of all the speculation and all the methods. When history by itself fails or refuses to "become a science," the old desire spurs an attempt to graft upon history such neighboring knowledge as wears the aspect of science. It is the theory of that effort and the difficulties met in practice that must now be examined so as to see on what terms the ologies of our day can be of use to History, should we find that they are compatible with it.

1

The Question of Substance

The New Terminology: Convenient but Confused

Anybody who can read has been exposed to history in some form. It need not be the book form, since history comes under our eyes in memorandums, reports, pamphlets, and the daily paper; and lately also to our ears by the broadcast word, as in the distant days of Herodotus. Nearly two centuries of such a mixed diet have formed the Western mind, so that the public of today absorbs historical matter as part of its workaday life, almost without noticing that it is history.* People's sense of time and their habits of comprehension require about each subject of interest an account of When? and In what sequence? The prose substance that furnishes the answers is familiar to all without a label; it is the ordinary style of business or journalism. The virtues of that substance at its best are: order, clarity, and directness; history uses no special language.

*The "importance" of history becomes a conscious idea when a practical argument arises; for example, when a textbook is attacked as unfair to national heroes or neglectful of minority groups; or again, when a moral objection to publishing the memoirs of Christine Keeler, the call girl in the Profumo scandal, is met by the plea that these memoirs matter "to history" ("Smut and History," *Daily Telegraph*, Oct. 17, 1969). In a kindred mood, statesmen and newspapers frequently signalize a particular event as "history being made." Importance of still another order inspired a firm of plumbing manufacturers to send five of its experts to Europe for a tour of "great historic baths" (*International Herald-Tribune*, Sept. 30, 1969).

It is in competition with this commonplace product—and lately in doctrinaire opposition to it—that psycho-history offers its works with the assurance that they embody a new discipline which justifies a distinctive name. The public is used to taking such christenings as authorized, which is one reason why the term psycho-history has so soon come to prevail. The compound fits easily into the growing class of words beginning in *psycho-*, of which the latest Webster lists 140—exactly twice as many as in the previous edition thirty-five years earlier.

A special label is needed, according to the advocates and practitioners, because psycho-history is not to be a mere addition or incorporation of psychological data in the writing of history, but a fusion in which the two constituents are modified each by the other. We are thus to expect, under a name ending in *-history*, not simply new knowledge but a different substance.

Yet even before we come to test this promise by close reading, we cannot help noticing that the hyphened name lacks precision. It is applied, for example, to Erik Erikson's *Young Man Luther*, which is not history but biography, and also to studies of mental types or social institutions, which are neither biography nor history, but something difficult to distinguish from previous sociological, psychiatric, or anthropological reports, all of which have always contained historical description in layers thick or thin. This uncertain usage warrants the conclusion that "psycho-history" actually stands for a broad attempt to juxtapose findings from any of the behavioral sciences with selected portions of history.

But the innovators tend to ignore their own diversity and try to pit in single combat a new discipline, or an interdisciplinary discipline, against what they call "traditional" or "conventional" history—as if history did not exist in many kinds and traditions. There is a paradox about the demand for interdisciplinary history, coming as it does from the specialists who in an earlier day worked so hard to separate from history the materials of their new sciences. The challengers do not seem aware that although history has no conventions but that of using the common tongue, its name and quality cannot be altered by fiat or confiscated at pleasure. These many confusions obscure the central issue, which is not whether history can or should use the findings of other branches of learning, but whether historians should allow the substance of their work to be modified by any intrusion of "method" whatever.

They might at first blush be inclined to accept the proposal on historical, evolutionary grounds. The attempt to rescue Clio from pitiable maidenhood by artificial insemination they know is nothing new. The exhortations to become a science are an old nineteenth-century habit. These precedents suggest that perhaps the time has come for a noble abdication. The heirs apparent are heartened by the proliferation of would-be sciences, to which our hopeful culture gives acceptance and support for mere striving and promise, the promise not of simple knowledge but of transferable knowledge: if two and two make four in this latitude, the same result will hold in every latitude. For the two and two history must be ransacked; the sum will be worked out by method. It is obviously hard to resist the imperialism of the scientific world-view which, coupled with the will to control, has produced all the eager ologies. And it would be hard-*hearted* to rebuff the aspirations they represent. As Burckhardt pointed out a hundred years ago, revolution and human perfectibility authorize the work of analysis for manipulation, not excluding that of the human mind: it has become the fashion, he said, "to trace the psyche of one's fellowmen; the great document of this is Lavater's work on physiognomy."[1]

The New Substance and Its Properties

Present-day psycho-historians may not relish the idea of intellectual descent from physiognomy and phrenology, but there it is, embedded in plain history. Let them take comfort in the thought that they bring to the workshop a very different material for fusion with history. To sample the characteristics of that new material, it is convenient to refer again to Professor Langer's essay in which he suggests a treatment of the Black Death in the light of depth psychology. In the eight pages devoted to this topic, Professor Langer speaks of repression (of unbearable fears), unconscious guilt (due to infantile repression of sexual and aggressive drives), and regression (to "infantile concepts") whenever man is overwhelmed by "unfathomable powers" such as great plagues.

This linking of familiar facts with psychoanalytic ideas is to help us understand the Middle Ages' resort to magic, fear of witchcraft, and waves of religious feeling. A generality is offered: "Death-dealing epidemics like those of the late Middle Ages were bound to produce a religious revival." And, earlier: "None of the commentators . . . have traced . . . the connection between the great and constantly recurring epidemics and the state of mind of much of Europe at that time. Yet this relationship would seem to leap to the eye."[2]

One readily sees how a full treatment of the subject would develop and what formulations it would offer the reader. There would be a study of documents to connect expressions of guilt more closely with the recourse to magic and religion. And any generality about fears and religion would be strengthened by a "control" study, based on records from periods and places relatively free of plagues, and therefore marked by less witchcraft and religion.

This is a program of ordinary historical research, assuming the right evidence to be there. In that research, clearly, no new method would be at work, only common sense and previous knowledge of the period. The "psychodynamic" element therefore resides in two things: (1) the hypothesis as to the source of deeper explanation and (2) the psychoanalytic terminology for description.

Now let us suppose the search for evidence successful, that is, rewarded by abundant documents, how —except for phraseology—will the account differ from earlier ones, in which the "state of mind of the Middle Ages" was related to: popular ignorance, superstitious fears, pagan survivals, the power of rumor, inadequate science, and strong institutional religion? The very words *superstitious, ignorant, geocentric, terrorized, priest-ridden* are so many psychological diagnoses. Plagues (and why not famines and wars as well?) obviously reinforce anxieties; there is no need of depth psychology to tell us that. As for the psychological tie between calamities and the sense of guilt, it was known to Job's friends, who analyzed his situation accordingly.

Tentatively, then, we may say that the proposed treatment of the Black Death, in its successful, documented form, would not supply a new kind of history, a sample of a new discipline; it would supply a restatement, with diagnoses added in technical language, of a fairly well-understood situation. But in so doing it would alter the substance of history in two ways. It would relegate description to the secondary role of support for diagnosis (this would be especially true if the "incidents" and other evidences were tabulated); and it would substitute technicalities for common speech.

In history proper, for reasons that will be shown later, the presence of untechnical language, the absence of jargon, are required. The historian, like the lawyer, is a critic of words, and he finds that in much recent psycho-history—for example in the pages summarized a moment ago—the vocabulary defeats its own ends. The reason is not that the words are unfamiliar, but that they are disparate and used without strictness. In short, the matter of history has been subordinated to a specialism which on reflection does not sustain its claim.

In this mixture we may still keep a grip on the relation between mundane fact and the minds affected by it. But in some works of psycho-history worldly facts tend to disappear after they have stimulated diagnosis. The substance of history is transmuted into subliminal mental states. Thus a sympathetic reviewer of a psycho-historical study of President Nixon was constrained to point out that "Mr. Nixon's 'overreaction' to the rejections [by the Senate] of Judges Haynsworth and Carswell may not need to be explained as 'projection' of 'one's own aggressive and nasty impulses' onto 'others'; . . . one could conclude just as easily that when Mr. Nixon announced in bitter tones that he wasn't going to subject any more Southerners to 'malicious character assassination,' he was simply trying to appease his Southern constituents."[3]

A further alteration of substance results from another ambiguity in psycho-history, not dependent on the loose application of psychology, but intrinsic and reflected in its very name. Unlike, say, economic history, psycho-history is not *of the psyche* as the other is *of economics*. What it means is: "psychologizing with the aid of history." And the first term in the compound word undermines the second. Once the character of a man or group has been diagnosed and described by psycho-history, man or group no longer has a real history in the sense that we may expect true novelty. Rather, events in the world illustrate how the agent behaves. In strictness he ought not to be called *agent* at all. This objection to a term misplaced has nothing to do with the undoubted fact that individual and national behavior shows constancy: men have habits. But they are not automatons. The question, then, is whether psycho-history, seeking the mechanism, allows us to believe in the reality of change by conscious means for conscious ends. Any other belief is alien to the nature of history, for its subject-matter is *res gestae*, things done; the activities of men, not the processes of physics. And since the historian, psycho- or plain, is not likely to discuss the philosophical difference between activity and process, the reader can only know what he is being shown—agents or puppets—if the language of description is clearly of one kind, the language of determinism or of freedom.

Take a valuable psychiatric study such as "Symbolic Aspects of Presidential Assassination." Its stated assumption is that "threats and gestures of assassination are symbolic acts and have meanings of which the actor is unaware. As symbols they may be studied in the context of language or communication. In this approach, the meaning of the act depends not only on its form and intrinsic content, but on its anticipated consequences, on the circumstances in which it is carried out, and on the relationship and social roles, real and putative, of the participants in the communication."[4] What follows is a report on actual and potential assassins and an analysis of what the presidency may signify to the unbalanced minds that plan or act out the killings.

The makings of this paper are taken from the social and political history of the United States since 1906 as well as from biography, that of each president and medical case. But the resulting work is psychiatry and not history. There is no fusion of interests; none was intended, and none possible. It is doubtful whether any historian dealing with the presidents or the presidency could make use of the findings. They have to do with the abstract idea of a head of state and with the danger arising from socially isolated individuals who may look upon the president as embodying a powerful "community from which they are excluded, or again as a mother-figure [*sic*]."*

"Studies" versus Histories

Since a presumption in favor of anything that promises to bring light is always in order, one must push beyond this negative illustration and try to imagine its opposite, in which a comparable handling of historical fact might serve the ends of history. Suppose again that the expanded study of medieval fears had gone beyond a mere restatement in psychological terms and shown a repeated connection between piety or superstition and plagues. The marshaled evidence would not leave the historian unmoved. He would say that here was an indicative—not a necessary—condition of which history should take note. But after scanning the report in which the demonstration was made, he would also say that he had in hand, not a piece of history of a new kind, but a piece of psychology—or sociology or anthropology. Its novelty would lie in one of these fields, for having reached its goal with the aid of historical in place of living materials. It would not be less valuable on that account—and possibly valuable to history. But once again, the book or article, however suggestive of an epithet or a paragraph in some future history, would

*But see below (p. 69n.) a medical study by the same author, the results of which would be easily absorbed into the substance of history and would affect important judgments of persons and events.

not consist of historical substance, would not be *a history of* anything.*

Such a judgment is confirmed by some of the younger practitioners who are praised as makers of the new history. For example, Professor Stanley Elkins, the author of *Slavery: A Problem in American Institutional Life,* denies that his brilliant book "was designed as a 'history' of slavery. It does not pretend to be a history, in either the extended or limited sense. Other scholars have produced historical studies far more thorough in compass than anything I could hope to do. The present study is merely a 'proposal.' It proposes that certain kinds of questions be asked in future studies of the subject that have not been asked in previous ones. . . . [M]y own study has been limited, perhaps seriously, by those questions which have seemed particularly pressing to me."[5] Nothing could be more judicious or candid, and the title of the work bears out the disclaimer. Who would wish to confuse the study of a "problem in institutional life" with a history?

The rejoinder to that question is: "What does the name matter?" It matters as does any false identification. If "studies" in the behavioral sense are taken as histories in the literal sense, the substitution will deprive the public (including students) of a product for which there is no substitute. This pattern is familiar in our workaday life, where the loss is concealed by a spoken or tacit assurance that the new product, being *different,* is *better* than the old, more scientific and up to date.

*Mr. John Demos, an "interdisciplinary" historian, makes the point when he says of his reliance on anthropologists: "The approach they follow differs strikingly from anything in the historical literature. Broadly speaking, the anthropological work is far more analytic, striving always to use materials on witchcraft as a set of clues or 'symptoms' " ("Underlying Themes in the Witchcraft of Seventeenth-Century New England," *American Historical Review* 75 [June 1970]: 1312).

This form of technological eclipse is not even so favorable to behavioral studies as might be thought, because their purview, closely linked to current concerns, tends to shift rapidly and widely. Sociologies and anthropologies follow fashion as much as the physical sciences and much more than history. Perhaps its alleged conservatism helps to keep it on an even keel. Indeed an historian is sometimes tempted to think that the various new genres cling to the name history to give a semblance of unity to the diffuse enterprise. Else why not ditch the word and coin a new term altogether?

In this scholarly shuffling one clear word would not be enough to dispel confusion; but it is a welcome example of what ought to be the rule when, on the subject of slavery again, Professor Genovese, a trained historian, tells his reader: "This book tries to do three complementary things: to extend an analysis of the society of the slave South presented earlier; to contribute to a rapidly unfolding discussion of the comparative study of modern slave societies; and to offer some suggestions for the development of the Marxian interpretation of history."[6] In other words: two contributions to sociology and one to methodology. History supplies the materials (as it might to anyone—a novelist or a politician), but they are to be used in the purely analytic mode, in the service of typology and technique.

When in fulfilling his program the writer comes to the question of "the slaveholder's philosophy," one wonders whether he will seize a plausible opportunity for psycho-history. He does not.[7] He knows how others have used psychoanalytic terms on his topic: "Guilt feelings reside deep in the individual psyche." But he concludes: "The guilt complex thesis is not necessarily wrong, it is irrelevant."[8] We take note, then, that an analytic, comparative, sociological historian, who wishes to define rather than to narrate, may decline to use the psychology in vogue and even considers it irrelevant.

This option, while it detracts from the claim to unique insight advanced by psycho-history, has the further effect of making any fusion of substance with history seem premature and presumptuous. Until such special studies are more assured, their promises of marriage or summonses to adoption must be viewed with extreme reserve: current concubinage may well suffer the fate of all *liaisons dangereuses.*

Certainty through Numbers

What have we learned so far? That *psycho-* prefixed to *history* can stand for various combinations of technical materials with historical and contemporary questions and must result in marked alterations of the substance of history; that the "mind" which embraces slavery or witchcraft may be disclosed by other means than depth psychology; and that, as the founding father suggested, the "next assignment" includes consultation with sociology and demography as well as psychology. Historians, accordingly, have offered the public books on such subjects as: *Wayward Puritans: A Study in the Sociology of Deviance* (Kai T. Erikson, 1966); *A Little Commonwealth: Family Life in Plymouth Colony* (John Demos, 1970); *White over Black: American Attitudes toward the Negro, 1550–1812* (Winthrop D. Jordan, 1968). In France also, similar preoccupations have inspired the work of Lucien Febvre, Ignace Meyerson, Robert Mandrou, and others, who promote what is known as *la psychologie historique.*

The recurrent use of psychology to characterize these fluid concerns deserves a moment's thought. It is evident that all the studies which deal with men's activities are branches of psychology. Even that which seems the most material, economics, ranks high among the mental or subjective. And none of the rest

—sociology, anthropology, sexology, linguistics, political science, demography—is detachable from psychology. With man as student and subject, how could it be otherwise? Bad times, inflation, stock-market slumps are molded out of psychological material. So are human institutions. In history, the tale of wars, panics, bubbles, and religions, the periods of moral laxity or artistic flowering are psychological phenomena—and demography as well: the birthrate goes up some months after a city blackout, and darkness is not the only cause.

But even when we have rediscovered mind at the center of our life, we have not explained the present urge to define "the mind" of this or that class, period, or institution—the mind of the slaveholder, the wayward puritan, the witch-hunter, the fascist crowd, or the petty bourgeois. It is a search for a collective mind, a uniform mind, a unit mind. The new effort resembles the painstaking work of nineteenth-century anthropologists to ascertain racial traits once and for all. The continuing purpose is to identify (i.e., see as identical) elements easier to grasp and handle than the miscellaneous contents of history.

Our examples have shown that psycho-history brings about this fundamental alteration: events and agents lose their individuality and become illustrations of certain automatisms. It is only a step from this way of perceiving to that of the statistician. And we find, sure enough, that in the behavioral studies linked to history the main interest shifts from things done to their net effect, and especially to that effect measured in numbers.

How unlike history in substance is the work of students who use history for such purposes* may be seen by mere inspection, without reading a word. One page

*"To find fresh answers" (to social questions) said the *New York Times* headline (July 3, 1971) over the report of findings in the new *Journal of Interdisciplinary History*. Diagrams and charts were reproduced.

will show tables and graphs or again a diagram in dots, crosses, and other marks, headed "Computer-Prepared Map of Violent Incidents in France, 1840–1844"—while on the opposite page is a geometrical outline of France, also crossed and dotted, showing the incidence of the incidents. Positive and negative numbers to three decimals express the absolute values applying to each of the "levels of violence," side by side with a frequency distribution.[9] An historian need feel no distaste whatever at this use of history; rather, he rejoices that the ancient urge to record events leads later on to such refined methods for distilling their supposed essence. But he knows as his eye ranges across a chart in all directions that he is not *reading history*.

It may occur to some that the distinction merely expresses the stiffness in the reader's mental joints. With a little practice the historian could learn to take in the gist of violence in France from crosses and decimals just as well as from a paragraph of prose—and more exactly. Such a hope will not stand a moment's reflection: narrated instances coupled with a verbal summary of effects strike different nerves and evoke different images from those brought into play by the ratiocinative perception of graphs and figures.

Can Rhetorics Be Mixed?

This issue of form and substance is frequently approached by quantitative historians, then for some reason run away from. The editors of *History as Social Science* remark that "the historian as social scientist knows that tables of statistics do not scan well. They break the rhythm of the text, and comments on numerical matters are often tedious . . ."[10] It need not necessarily be so, and in any case that is not the objection: tables are digestible and welcome if their size and contents help support or illustrate the text and not the other way around. The count of some material fact that can be counted, such as population, tons of coal, or miles of road, suggests size or change of size, exemplifies rate of change. Numbers are unassimilable as historical matter if they *constitute* the message, and especially if they pretend to *measure* something not really homogeneous, such as violence.

Not only will the relations of dates and "amounts" not replace judgments and conclusions stated in words, but it is also an illusion to suppose that the point they make is unmistakable and exact. For the question of exactitude is more complicated than common opinion imagines when it assumes that numbers=exact, words=inexact. The idea of exactitude implies a relation; we ought to say "exact to" something, as we say "correspond to." It is by due rhetoric that a history is exact, communicates its truth, imparts the precise fact found by the researcher and precisely set by him in the context where its just weight will be correctly felt.

Nor should the chart-and-table advocate delude himself that his devices are not also a rhetoric. They impress in a unique way, and as a craftsman choosing and using them he is an impressionist. Professor J. H. Plumb, who with his usual irony applauds innocent play with numbers, does so on this very ground of rhetoric: "We are becoming a numerate society: almost instinctively there seems now to be a greater degree of truth in evidence expressed numerically than in any literary evidence, no matter how shaky the statistical evidence, or acute the observing eye. It is often not the numbers that speak the truth, rather there is a quicker acceptance of them in ourselves—almost an excitement."[11]

And he goes on to give an instance from Fernand Braudel's book *The Mediterranean,* in which the author "spends pages calculating the average income in ducats of the agricultural worker. The evidence is slender, uncertain, disparate: the margins of error, Braudel admits, are so very great that the calculations are almost meaningless. And the upshot is that [the] . . . workers lived on the margin of subsistence, which of course we knew from scores of literary sources. Nevertheless, these juggled ducats seem to clinch the argument more firmly."[12]

This remarkable confession tells us much about the contemporary search for a persuasive myth. Assuming that it has been found in numbers, it does not follow that their promiscuous use with other forms of magic, namely words, is permissible. The truth that the historian conveys by his skillful rhetoric may well be damaged by the kind of tables or the form of charts that impose on the mind a radically different sort of attention and movement. In words we attend to complex wholes; in figures we must think of collections of identical units in fixed ratios; in the former we pass from vision to vision at a steady pace; in the latter we stand and compare, back and fill as new relations occur to us, not hinted at by the numerical author.

The skepticism appropriate to each kind of perception differs too, and this has importance, for reading history is not only an esthetic experience but also a critical exercise. In verbal history the critical sense acts upon the pattern displayed—is it too neat? And on the motives alleged—are they improbable? Whereas in quantitative history, despite the preliminary account of how things were classified and computed and adjustments made, the skeptical eye scans the method more than the results. In spite of greater "certainty" in quantified results, statistical technique is subject to endless argument among professionals, as are among thoughtful laymen the validity of the unit used and the feasibility of measurement in the given conditions. Professor Plumb's case, it is clear, presupposes a love of clever deception. As in going to a puppet show, the viewer relishes the figures that he has every reason to disbelieve. But there are other minds in whom it is not "almost an instinct" to be impressed by numbers; and this, not because of inability to handle them, but because of a sharp sense of the gap between the concrete world and the abstraction of quantity.

At any rate, in history properly so called, historical statements must predominate over the rest, must surround them and subdue them to the purposes of historical knowledge. If "historical statement" needs further illustration, perhaps the shortest ever made will suffice: "Veni, vidi, vici" is an historical statement. "The mainspring of his character was conquest" is a psychological statement. "The net effect of his career was more constructive than destructive by far" is a sociological statement. The three may follow one after the other in a piece of history; but if they are separated into kinds, so as to be totted up and analyzed by a student indifferent to events as such, then we have a quite other product of intellect. It may have its own virtues, indeed must have them to hold our attention; but it cannot replace the knowledge that history affords, or by "fusion" improve it, or by subordinating it to formula dispossess the discipline of history from its own domain.

2

The Question of Method

The Search for the Diagnostic

Psycho-history in its several forms lays claim to two kinds of importance. One lies in results; the second in method, which validates the first. But even a brief survey of the field shows that no single method is to be found in the works deemed most representative of the new departure. More serious still, nothing that may be called methodical procedure is apparent. What does appear is that one or another of the contemporary psychologies has yielded conclusions—or more often, as we saw in Professor Langer's illustration, formulas and terms—which the historical researcher makes use of in writing up his results. Every student feels free to draw on any idiom of the behavioral sciences that he chooses. Professor Elkins, it will be remembered, proposed an answer to the "institutional problem" of slavery. He had recourse to depth psychology for the purpose and—as he points out—his solution came to him by way of a metaphor: "the mind of the South" is likened to the mind of a man in a concentration camp. These two hypothetical minds taken as one mind are then analyzed, first by the psychological method of Freud; next, that of Harry Stack Sullivan; and finally that of the propounders of "role psychology." The successive analyses are elaborate; they impress the reader with the author's desire to reach positive results and at the same time to make a point about method. Professor Elkins is so exacting of himself that when he thinks he has found what he sought he can state it with a modest confidence: "We thus have a potentially durable link between individual psychology and the study of culture."[1]

This affirmation goes beyond Freud's own cautious thought, which is not an argument against Professor Elkins: perhaps we progress. Yet it is well to recall Freud's words, because they refer to the use of analogy: "I would not say that . . . an attempt to apply psychoanalysis to civilized society would be fanciful or doomed to fruitlessness. But it behoves us to be very careful, not to forget that, after all, we are dealing only with analogies, and that it is dangerous, not only with men, but also with concepts, to drag them out of the region where they originated and have matured."[2]

Analogies and metaphors obviously do not come by method but by inspired assumption. Psycho-historical method, then, does not always rest directly on pure historical material, nor does it spring from it by strong suggestion as did Freud's thought from his clinical material. The idea of a mind damaged by life in a concentration camp could not have occurred to anyone as a metaphor before the invention of such camps in the Boer War, and is therefore not an irresistible image; it never struck those who observed or embodied the "mind" of the South.

The upshot of these reflections is that method, despite its reassuring sound, is in this particular application little more than the use of a suggestive comparison. One does not yet see how it can "solve an institutional problem." But let us go on. The "durable link," doubted by Freud but sought in modern inquiry, is of course the goal of the sociologist, who may find it by mass observation after the psychologist has indicated what to look for, thanks to his correct theory of personality. In Professor Elkins the theory is an amalgam made by him from Sullivan's interpersonal psychology and the later role-playing psychology. One can see why he could not be content with either alone: the self is the individual aspect of living man, who in society fulfills a role not uniquely his. But can it be said that a new method arises for historical interpretation when it has to rely on borrowings from two other methods? And where in methodology is one to fit Professor Genovese's debonair remark that the psychological base of the interpretation may be right but is irrelevant? The essence of method is singleness—of purpose, procedure, terminology, and definition. Without agreed details under each of these headings method is not transferable, that is, teachable and properly applicable to other cases.

Besides, the method must work when wanted. Historians of the ordinary kind are not insensible to the lure of finding a "durable link." They would respond warmly to the demonstration of even a tentative link. For example, at the Conference of 1971 mentioned in the Preface above, Professor Meyer Schapiro, the distinguished art historian, repeatedly called on the psycho-historians across the table to supply him with the link in a typical situation that has long puzzled him. Manuscripts can be dated by the recurrent change in the form of the handwriting. Why does a medieval scribe or a Renaissance lawyer's clerk "suddenly" change his hand, after which others follow suit? Or do they shift in clusters, gradually? Professor Schapiro received no help.

Part of the difficulty, perhaps, is to know what a satisfactory answer would be, and that is no doubt why the search for "method" goes on, in and out of as many ologies as give signs of seriousness and plausibility. Long before the late nineteenth-century sociologist Tarde, historians had observed the workings of social imitation and they knew how much can be accounted for by boredom and novelty-seeking. But the clue to the action of fashion leader upon follower remains where it was left by those who used to discuss the mutual fitness of innovation and receptivity.*

An Embarrassment of Riches

Even if the definition of "method" is loosened far enough to mean a free use of several methods, the question remains: "What guides the choice?" There are other psychologies and psychiatries than those derived from Freud. The latest edition of Woodworth's classic *Contemporary Schools of Psychology*[3] lists seven broad tendencies long pursued and equally in repute. And since that survey, the phenomenologist psychology practiced at the Copenhagen Laboratorium has produced new findings that are now receiving respectful attention from American leaders of older schools.[4] Is it impossible to conceive that any or all of these eight kinds of teaching and their subdivisions have something to say about human motives and social action?

What *is* impossible to conceive is that a reader could encompass a paragraph, relevant to history though it be, that began: "Action potentials are to a large extent exercising an influence on my set when I perceive the behavior of another person and thereby influence what *sens* I shall perceive in a given material sequence. . . . We see how a perceived stamp creates a set so that behavior is experience . . . without any real *sens*."[5] Not until *sens*, "set," "stamp," and "action potentials" are household words will this valuable remark help "explain" (as in fact it does) why Woodrow Wilson and Clemenceau misunderstood each other at the Paris

*On this subject, see two classic essays by William James: "Great Men and Their Environment" and "The Importance of Individuals" (*The Will to Believe and Other Essays*, New York, 1897 ff.). The second essay is a brilliant refutation, with historical examples, of some objections provoked by the first.

Conference. An alternative still lower on the scale of concreteness would be to account for confusion at a conference by the explanation that "the empirical masking function for sinusoids in white noise is governed by fixed signal-to-noise ratios."[6] Such might be the observation of a physical psychologist, who has the advantage of being in a literal and not a metaphorical sense a user of method.

But fortunately, explanation in terms as technical as those is not indispensable to the historian. He has the means of *showing* Wilson and Clemenceau addressing each other out of their separate fogs, and can count on the reader's intimate experience of what confusion is.

This is not to say that the historian may not profit from the reading of such psychologies and pathologies as he is able to understand. Striking case histories can dispel prejudices that he does not suspect, physiological concomitants of behavior can be suggestive, new terms and definitions can reshape one's perceptions and refresh the awareness of complexity—the very word *Gestalt* restrains the tendency toward destructive analysis. And these things being true, one must amend Professor Langer's statement that classical and academic psychologies have nothing to teach the historian: all the reputable ones put him in touch with some aspect of the mind. But none furnish him with a method—a series of steps to be followed—that can be relied on to solve the unknowns of history. If, as we saw earlier, the "guilt thesis" can be right but irrelevant for Professor Genovese in his study of slavery, it can be irrelevant for all historians who so decide, about any institution or character.

True, some schools of psychology, past and present, have given currency to words and ideas which form a kind of shorthand so commonly used that we take the words themselves as explanation. But here again we are not in possession of a method. Understanding remains the task of the beholder; and perhaps the fullest understanding will come to one whose experience of the world keeps him from the delusion of thinking he holds the key to the riddle of the Sphinx when he reads "Oedipus complex," or any other phrase from any philosophy of the mind.

In such conditions of variability, of accidental usage, of absence of method, it cannot be said that a new type of history is born each time the vocabulary of psychology changes. Its objects and moral tone have been transformed again and again from pagan to Christian times and from deist to Marxist centuries. The history of Freudian psychoanalysis itself has gone through at least three phases in eighty years, finally branching out into as many sects as there are theorists and practitioners. Any attempt to establish a common denominator of doctrine would be difficult and vulnerable; so that, once more, the "method" of dynamic or depth psychology boils down to the vocabulary that has filtered out of successive teachings and hypotheses.

Is Biography the Place for Method?

To make entirely sure that no merit in psycho-history is being overlooked, one must not leave the subject of method without asking whether, all questions of history apart, depth psychology has not already gone a great way to light up the dark places of individual character. We saw that the "durable link" from psychology to social problems required the supposition that a society or its subgroups had a "mind," and this entailed difficulties of definition. But a person comes ready equipped with a mind, and doctors of the mind readily subject him to method, in the proper sense of a series of steps, of well-known operations and manipulations in orderly sequence. Hence the historical study of a person—biography—which has always called forth random psychological remarks, might be the true playground for a systematic tackling of the psyche.

Certainly the finest achievements so far credited to psycho-history are biographies, chief among them Erik Erikson's *Young Man Luther* and David Donald's *Charles Sumner.* Yet different as these two works are, there can be no mistaking them for applications of clinical method. They are simply lives in the modern mode. Both books are praiseworthy for reasons that invite the critic himself to psychologize: Mr. Erikson, a psychoanalyst, took pains to become a good historical researcher; and Mr. Donald, an historian, took pains to become a careful student of psychological doctrine. Add to this double preparation judgment and literary skill and you have two impressive studies.

No doubt, their selection of facts and the ideas that bind them in explanatory ways are not of a kind found in every biography. It can even be agreed that the importance given to psychoanalytic considerations in these two works, not written for specialists (for whose purposes full case histories would be required), is a bold departure that marks a date. But that is not the issue. The issue is whether we have been given here something more rigorous than other accounts, thanks to the application of a new method. In theory, method guarantees results. But other "depth" biographies have not fared so well as these two at the hands of the critics, who seem able to counter the conclusions born of method by facts drawn from the public record.[7]

Now the "point of view" has always played a great part in biography, if only because the attraction of the subject for the writer often derives from the presence of materials suited to the exercise of a special interest: the soldier writes about Napoleon as military commander; the doctor as an obese pyknic with Malta fever. Technical specialization in biography had already gone far before the claims of psycho-history were voiced. Many "determinants" had been tried: medical, phrenological, racial, sexual, optometric, genetic, economic, criminal, or theological; and even where explanation was not pushed to the point of determinism, there was—to use Professor Elkin's words—a clear conceptual framework for personality analysis.* To allude to these precedents, some of which are obsolete, infamous, or absurd, is not to cast aspersions on present-day psycho-biography. It is but to look at biography historically and remind ourselves that the inherent interest of great lives is such that it can survive concentration on certain facts at the expense of others. Explanation by a single cause may make a "viewy" biography short-lived or usefully suggestive; it does not make it more true thanks to method.

Counting Is Also a Linear Mode

The one-sidedness of the "special study" occurs wherever method is deliberately applied, including the method of counting. In order to count one must have similar units, preferably "given" ready-made in experience rather than made up by an act of definition for the purpose of the study. Thus population can be counted, though with enormous difficulty and uncertainty, as the margin of error in the United States census-taking demonstrates. The money value of imports and exports, the number of copies of a book sold

*Dr. William B. Ober, for example, has written entrancing "medical lives" of Keats and Boswell, and his "Thomas Shadwell" is a model of insight and knowledge effecting a rehabilitation of the poet damned by Dryden ("Thomas Shadwell: His Exitus Revis'd," *Annals of Internal Medicine* 74 [January 1971]: 126 ff.). Even the egregious Dr. George M. Gould, whose *Biographic Clinics* (6 vols., Philadelphia, 1903–9) discovered ophthalmic astigmatism as the ubiquitous cause and curse of genius, makes some interesting observations. Similarly, the work of W. H. Sheldon on body types, though never generally accepted, draws attention to relationships that could supply evocative words in historical portraiture.

within a span of time, the number of cars registered or manufactured are also discoverable and usable in the writing of history. But whenever the unit is not "given" and must be established by definition and sorted by judgment, the "objective" character of the method recedes and arbitrariness, which is the negation of method, steps in. Thus the statistics of crime, as the best statisticians tell us, are extremely unreliable. Between the dishonest falsifications (reports showing fewer crimes, to prove police efficiency) and automatic falsifications (divergent definitions, plea bargaining, etc.) it is not possible to know what the returns correspond to, let alone what they mean.* Here as in psycho-history the mingling of methods (in the plural) renders Method illusory.

Aware, perhaps, of this difficulty, the quanto-historian will prefer to measure rather than to count and will believe himself all the more scientific for doing so. True measurement differs from counting in that it deals with a homogeneous substance, using a defined portion of it as a standard for gauging the rest—as in the familiar instances of the foot, the ounce, the pint, or the British Thermal Unit. But where in human affairs do we find homogeneous material? Language uses abstractions—violence, divorce, revolutionary propaganda—but these are only names for a group of particular acts, which nothing guarantees to be homogeneous.

In history, similar terms correctly applied can yet deceive. Even when they seem to denote a firm identity—slavery is slavery the world over, isn't it? any slave is his master's chattel, surely?—the reality does

*See "A Critical View of the Uniform Crime Reports," by Dr. Sophia M. Robison in the *New York Statistician*, October 1966: these reports are ". . . a shaky foundation for estimating the quantity or quality of crime or delinquency in the U.S. . . . Erroneous impressions are created . . . partly because of classification and partly because of the method of calculation of rates of incidence" (p. 3).

not conform to the verbal abstraction. Slavery in the United States differed in almost all important respects from its nominal counterpart in the early Roman Empire, and both still more from slavery in the Ottoman Empire, where the nearly 100,000 slaves were the Establishment, the elite, the rulers, the army. The sultan himself was son of a slave, not by accident but by constitutional law. This unique system of recruiting the state's religious enemies and training them under duress to govern the state worked for almost half a millennium, in defiance of "human nature" and of the psycho- and quanto-historical minds.

The best, most manageable attempts to create homogeneity by excluding what is unlike a defined standard still tend toward the arbitrary. Thus in recent studies of the courts, the entity "durable case" (i.e., long-lasting) was devised. It permits the investigator to obtain figures possibly helpful in stirring up reform sentiment, but it gives no measure of the inefficiency of justice, for delay is not a uniform substance produced entirely by court procedure. The illness of a defendant, the corruption of a prosecutor, the complexity of a bankruptcy may make a case drag on without help from faulty administration. Knowing this, the quantifier will want to eliminate the disparate. He does so by applying a criterion made up ad hoc and is again—with the best will and conscience—arbitrary.

Counting and measurement not only disregard the dissimilar; they also tempt to a mental side-slip: when the subject-matter is elusive, go after something close to it—or thought to be close. For example, a study of genius skirts the difficulty of saying what genius is by taking the persons listed in *Who's Who*—an incredible substitution, almost sure to exclude genius from the study. This notorious case is buried in the dim past of fifty years ago but the legerdemain is not buried with it, as will appear in chapter 5.

Now if to avoid false identification and false homogeneity each case is studied for its characteristics, then we have abandoned measurement and method and returned to the practice of history.* At that point the direct judgment of good observers familiar with the evidence is as useful as the roundabout method—and more discriminating.

The same objection holds against the practice of so-called model-building, borrowed for history from the science of economics. The model is designed by induction of a sort and then successively "verified" by applying it to historical situations about which much is known. Thus the model that posits national war as the result of inner disequilibrium is applied to the condition of France in 1870 and behold, a dire lack of equilibrium is found among the groups supporting the regime of Napoleon III. Whether internal dissension was at its peak in that year, or (if not) why the national disequilibrium did not topple into war earlier or later, cannot be answered without the quantifiers. It is not likely that they will be restrained by diffidence from giving figures on such impalpable things as mutual hostility, or by the knowledge that in economics itself, where the elements naturally lend themselves to numerical expression, some of the best minds have declared their distrust of figures and models.† In detailing the conditions of war, mere historians are of course content with the old maxim that authoritarian regimes in trouble at home often try to rally support by a foreign war. What the model adds to the maxim is the shadow of Method.

*Attention to "the characteristics of each case" does not rule out—on the contrary—the kind of comparative treatment which illuminates by looking into similarity *and* difference. The writer of these words is a co-founder of the *Journal of Comparative History*.

†See H. O. Stekler, "Forecasting with Economic Models, an Evaluation," *Econometrics* 36 (1968); Oskar Morgenstern, *On the Accuracy of Economic Observations*, 2d ed. (Princeton, 1963); and Ely

Seven Regretful Objections

The proponents of *History as Social Science* express surprise that historians appear "hostile to any kind of normalization of research procedure" and "resent the use of a word like re-tooling." There is, one hopes, no word *like* re-tooling, but the historian's objection is not perverse. It expresses a refusal to play at the laboratory life, where tools—material instruments—are indispensable. As for "normalization," it seems better suited to the factory even than to the laboratory, where free invention is as much needed as routine.* And so the historian remains skeptical—of tools in the metaphoric sense, of "method" in the boastful sense. The reasons may seem disconnected yet they relate to the situation as it is:

1. Method in psycho-history is much talked about but seldom seen. No description is given of the step and the result that led to the next step and result and so to the conclusion. Anything short of this is not method but the uncontrolled use of a vocabulary.

2. Which method or whose method yields valid psycho-historical conclusions does not receive treatment, either. A mingling of methods is tacitly held permissible, though again without any formal indication of their compatibility or of the manner of their

---

Devons, *Essays in Economics* (London, 1961). The last-named writer speaks of the professional habit of conceding error in statistical counts and then proceeding as if there were no error: "This attitude to error and unreliability is implicit in most econometric analysis. . . . There has been much theoretical examination in recent years of the meaning and significance of what we measure . . . and most of it leads to the conclusion that, except in very special and unusual circumstances, it is not possible to give any significant meaning to index numbers of real national income, production, or price" (p. 112).

*This association of ideas is not out of place: a "new" English historian, Mr. Keith Thomas, looks forward to "the age of the historical factory" (*Times Literary Supplement*, April 7, 1966, p. 275).

combining, with one another and with the ways of the historian.

3. How the method-user passes from individual psychology to the "mind" of an age or group is not clear. At this point the difficulties inherent in positing a homogeneous reality begin for the psycho-historian and the quanto-historian alike: how does the former *define and analyze* the entity he assumes; how does the latter *define and measure* it?

4. These difficulties exist because the two types of investigator imbued with method ask themselves questions essentially non-historical and profess to give them precise answers of a scientific kind: the fixed connection between stated conditions (Professor Elkins's "durable link"; Professor Langer's pestilence-religion correlation), or the measure of such connections in numbers and graphs relating to violence, public opinion, or the standard of living in some past period.

5. The historian, aware of his own taxing duty to reproduce in another mind the exact pattern in which he has organized his findings, doubts the capacity of the graphic-quantitative mode of representation for truth-telling. He is unfavorably struck by the angular rigidity of graphic and numerical statements, coming on top of the extremely "soft" manner of defining, classifying, and admitting or excluding the data.

6. The method implied in the use of models partakes of the definiteness of numbers; its additional defect is that it winds up in tautology, saying in abstract and pompous terms what historians formerly described in concrete and simple ones.

7. The final objection to method for history-writing is that method limits the mind—or it is not method. Method prescribes ahead of time the operations of thought upon its material. This can be very useful. As Whitehead pointed out, the method of algebra enables

you to calculate easily and correctly when you do not in the least know what you are doing. But to justify the mind's self-denial, the method must be both foolproof and accurately used. None of the new historians would claim that their method, whichever it may be, is foolproof. Some might maintain that they use it accurately; but in the absence of a demonstration, that is, a systematic account of the principles and devices used, each being shown to have validity through previous verification by results, the claim of accurate use cannot be judged.

Feeling the force of these objections, the mere historian can only conclude that he had better keep his mental activity unrestricted by methods—at least so long as those available do not meet the standard set by the definition of Method itself.

3

The Question of Evidence

The Sense of Fact and the Lure of Inference

Doubts about number and method as they occur in the improved historical genres bring the critic of psycho-history face to face with the *un*improved historian's greatest strength: his regard for evidence. What do I know? How do I know it? are challenges continually buzzing in his ears.* The answers that his discipline requires spring from particulars perceived, not from the operation of any system. The contrast with the workings of psycho-history is therefore marked. The psycho-historian uses the common historian's facts to infer and assert others. In weighing the worth of these second-grade facts, one need not go into the logical status of psychoanalytic principles: some are hypotheses, others are circular arguments: let them be equally accepted as heuristic devices often successful in therapy and consider only whether they can serve history by supplying facts and truths hitherto overlooked.

Facts and truths differ from suggestion, speculation, interesting possibility. Without inquiry into the nature of a fact and of its perception by the mind, it is clear that an attested fact and a suggestive possibility belong to separate orders of belief. One is evidence, the other is atmosphere. With proper safeguards these orders may be juxtaposed, but they do not communicate. X was

*While at work the historian probably puts the two questions in reverse order and in somewhat different words, but they amount to the same thing: What is the evidence? What does it mean?

born by a Caesarian operation; so much is shown by the doctor's statement, the hospital records, the accepted tradition in the family: so far, evidence. That X owed to this manner of birth his fearlessness as a child, his daring as a soldier and mountaineer in adult life, is a mere likelihood, a possibility, not a truth. There is no evidence for it, and there is counter-evidence in the attested fact that other men, born in the normal way, were also fearless and daring.

This attempt at interpreting character rests on a very loose connection, such as persons without pretensions or training casually make. The psycho-historian professes to be more exacting and is confident that he draws on wider and deeper knowledge. An example from the conference on psycho-history of April 1971 will make this clear, even though the speaker's remarks were impromptu. They were also lucid, well-organized, and unquestioned by any of the psycho-historians present. Their purpose was to illustrate the diagnostic power of depth psychology. The speaker* rehearsed the way in which analysts form inductive generalizations from repeated observations of their patients and went on to an historical application. A friend of his, interested in Rousseau, showed him the famous Venetian chapter in the *Confessions* (Book VII), where Rousseau is discomfited in front of a beautiful girl whom he passionately desired, because (says Rousseau) she was marred by the congenital lack of one nipple. The analyst then remembered reading that Rousseau suffered from enuresis as well as from a sexual malformation (hypospadias). The diagnosis promptly followed: by unconscious identification, Rousseau projected his defect upon the girl.

The historian at once notes that the conclusion asserts two facts, one about Rousseau's mind, the other about the girl's physical conformation. Rousseau gives

*Dr. Douglas Bond, of the Case–Western-Reserve Medical School.

a rather different explanation of the event. He recalls feelings which he experienced a little while before he saw the girl's breast and which its sight revived. The fact of *his* deformity is known to us independently, from ocular evidence on record. But if the autobiographical account is to be questioned, what the historian wants to know is whether the girl had one nipple or two—and for this also he wants independent evidence. He is not content to accept as fact the *possibility* that Rousseau "projected" and saw single where he should have seen double.

At times the historian, too, has to be content with a likelihood, but he is careful to state it as such. In the absence of documentary evidence he refuses to equate facts and inferences, ascertained particulars and inductive generalities. The inductions of psychoanalysis are not thereby made less valuable in psychology or therapy; it is their status *in history* that is dubious. And their unchallenged use in the learned give-and-take of a conference shows how they shape the opinions of a practitioner—psycho-history in the existential state.

Betrayal by Words and Analogies

The historian follows a different habit. He is always ready with negative instances that limit or destroy the possibilities drawn from induction. He can always think of alternative explanations. Since Rousseau was by no means uniformly impotent, the failure told by himself can have resulted from many circumstances other than those which a psychoanalyst likes to think virtually certain. Human actions—or inactions—depend on a rich mixture of motives; it is one of the functions of history to keep reminding us. When an historian or biographer uses a plausible inference to supply a suggestive touch, he takes care not to let it work upon his mind or the reader's to the point where surmise turns into fact. The *locus classicus* of the failure of the sense of fact is the discussion by Mr. F. W. Bateson of Dorothy Wordsworth's affection for her brother William, where a suspicion of incestuous love gradually turns into a certainty without further evidence.[1]

A tell-tale sign of such public- and self-deception is the use of weasel words.* Language does the work of suborning the witness. Thus in *The Mind of Adolf Hitler* one reads of "the fact that as a child he *must have* discovered his parents during intercourse. An examination of *the data* makes this conclusion *almost inescapable* [the data are some remarks not even hinting at such an event], and from *our knowledge* of his father's character and past history, it is *not at all improbable. It would seem* that his feelings on this occasion were very mixed."[2] The italicized words, not stressed in the original of course, amount to a blanket "may we not believe?" of the most treacherous kind. It leads the writer to ignore his own verbal hedging and to wind up with a supposed "occasion" when a conjectural "fact" produced certain "feelings," equally supposititious.†

Psycho-history is not bound by its theory to commit such grievous misdeeds. Many of its practitioners are trained historians and have shown their professional competence. But their attempts to reach a new certainty depend on mingling the degrees of belief—that which is consonant with their respect for evidence and that

*The revised edition of *Wordsworth: A Re-Interpretation* (1956) uses this device to retain the thesis summarized above. Where originally one read: "Wordsworth's purpose . . . is clear," the phrasing now is: "purpose is not known. Had he perhaps, realizing the dangers of the situation . . . ?" And again: "Wordsworth was undoubtedly fully aware . . ." becomes: "was probably fully aware." Adverbs and rhetorical questions permit insinuation with diminished responsibility.

†The late Bernard DeVoto, an indefatigable fact-hunter, had harsh words for this kind of imposture: "absolute bilge uncontaminated by the slightest perceptible filtrate of reality" (*Biography as an Art,* ed. James Clifford [London, 1962], p. 146).

which is drawn from clinical knowledge. This knowledge is generally second hand; it is the findings of others, reproduced in words. Since the findings are brought into history for diagnosis by way of formula, they affect the larger conclusions and not simply the isolated event, as to which the psycho-historian lacks the guide of experience. Everything he uses—his "tools," his "method," his "data"—is indirect and necessarily scant: the patient is absent, and the clues he may have left to his once living psyche are the product of chance. Diaries, letters, literary works form a random record, in which expressions of mood are more frequent than evidence of actions. "Dream-material" is extremely rare. Compared to the volume of data elicited under therapy and consciously directed at relevance and completeness by the analyst, this trickle from written remains seems almost negligible.*

Moreover, the historian's materials being static, not subject to cross-examination, they are often ambiguous. The psycho-historian has to make the most of the few points that in the light of theory he deems unmistakable. He is kept by the meager record—meager from his point of view—from following the preferred historical practice which, like that of the law, is to gather as many concurrent witnesses as possible.

And from these witnesses, both law and history want literal answers. The testimony of depth psychology is, on the contrary, metaphorical; it relies on symbol and analogy—yet another obstacle to establishing fact. Professor Elkins, in his book on slavery, is very much aware of this danger and he devotes some pages to defending "analogy as evidence."[3] His ground is that

*In the last essay he published, Freud wrote: "What we are in search of is a picture of the patient's forgotten years that shall be alike trustworthy and in all essential respects complete." "Constructions in Analysis" (Standard Edition of Freud's Works, ed. John Strachey, 23: 258).

metaphor is a recognized means of communication, which is true. But it does not follow that metaphor as such is trustworthy. The reader of metaphors cannot be expected to restrict his perception of likeness to the right features of the things compared. He may be on his guard as long as he sees the metaphor for what it is, but in analytic language as in any other the image soon merges with its object, the analogy with the reality, at which point the problem of evidence reappears.*

Take a common example of the "forgotten metaphor." It has become usual in our century to speak of great conquerors, the scourges of mankind, as Professor Langer did at the 1971 conference, namely as "pathological." On what evidence? Functionally and statistically, they seem to represent the norm. "Pathological" is a metaphor that passes for a description, but it only expresses our moral condemnation. And it does not promote straight thinking; for if the conquerors' pathological condition could be proved it would eliminate their moral responsibility, and then we could no longer condemn them: which way do we want to have it?

Introducing the Personal Equation

The phrase "personal equation" has been debased, but it has a scientific meaning, which is: a correction such as that which must be introduced into the observations of an ocular astronomer to compensate for the imperfection of his eyesight. The parallel defects of

*The words in the text above follow the short-cut of ordinary speech. Actually, analogy and metaphor proceed not from resemblance between objects but from parallels between relations—as A is to B, so C is to D; e.g., to say that nations are born, mature, and die is to say that as birth, growth, etc., are to an organism, so are the stated phenomena to nations. It is when analogy creates belief in a resemblance or in parallel relations other than those stated that fallacies flourish.

mind are not computable but they exist. Psycho-historians see others moved by unconscious forces that distort vision and compel strange behavior, but they assume themselves to be clear transmitters of light and judgment. Why is their vision of persons and events not blurred and skewed as well, and their interpretations forced upon them by dark needs rather than evidential reasons?

An unconscious determination to read the message of mute documents in a certain way meets no resistance—and "unconscious" here may range in meaning from "unaware" to the Unconscious, which is at work in psycho-historians too. How then assess Professor Leon Edel's interpretation of William James's character throughout the five volumes of the biography of Henry James? A powerful "sibling rivalry" animating the elder William against Henry is represented as a fact and an explanation. Alleged signs of jealous hostility confirm this "reading" until, near the end of the two great lives, sentences are quoted about Henry from a letter of William's that seem to put the case beyond doubt. Unfortunately, the full text of the letter, not given by the psycho-biographer, shows it to have been twisted and garbled to fit the long-held thesis. The tone and point of the document, its good-natured irony, are missed or suppressed in the endeavor to clinch a diagnosis.[4] Knowing the scholarly care and conscience of the biographer, one can only suppose that the distortion was unconscious in origin.

Bias also afflicts the ordinary historian, to be sure, but the safeguards against it are stronger, because the evidence to be sifted is in plain sight and the bias also. A writer may have political, religious, or esthetic prejudices that thwart his intellectual honesty; but they sooner or later disclose themselves, because he is not dealing in signs and metaphors. He can be challenged and asked to produce his sources, palpable, open to all.

The psycho-historian's proofs are not similarly transparent. He says: "I know; let me tell you." He assigns "projection" as a cause and who is to gainsay him? The scene he reports takes place in the depths, to which only he has access. Challenge him and he repulses you with his method, which gives him undiscussable insights; he has stepped off the common ground of evidence.

This objection applies not solely to interpretation but also to the events on which it is based. Access is cut off at the very point where the facts are said to be new and valuable. An incident in Freud's life and his generalization about it provide an apt example. After missing a train connection at Cologne, Freud analyzes the somewhat complicated series of events. It was a purposive error, he says, because he saw (and suppressed) clear indications of the way to his train.[5] But why is he correct in remembering that he saw the sign on the platform and blinded himself to it? Why is that memory itself not the error unconsciously determined? The data are beyond reach, and both the situation and its meaning, however useful to Freud's self-knowledge, can have no standing in history.

Skepticism, which includes a rare willingness to hold no opinion whatever on certain subjects, puts forth its irritating demand for open evidence on the very ground that Freud reaches after his anecdote: "Only for the most select and balanced minds does it seem possible to guard the perceived picture of external reality against the distortion to which it is otherwise subjected in its transit through the psychic individuality of the one perceiving it."[6] The theory and practice of the law, which in its evolution has done more than any other discipline to insure proper conditions for judgment, do not expect to work only with "select minds" and have made rules of evidence instead. History need not be as exclusionary as the law; but it does well to be guided by the psychological wisdom embodied in the safeguards of legal procedure.* Besides a lawyer-like care in the watch he keeps over his biases, the historian finds his chief bulwark against error in his passion for direct, reproducible evidence.

The Danger of Reading Signs

Skepticism about inference and possibility does not mean that the evidence preferred by the historian—documents, relics, monuments, traditions—is as it were radioactive: it does not send out unmistakable messages; it too must be interpreted; its one clear advantage over symbols and symptoms is that it is public. But for public debate and rational interpretation, evidence requires a prepared mind to receive it. The force of evidence, therefore, has an inward and individual face—the juryman's ability to make something of what he hears. On this important subject one would welcome a "psychology of credibility," a "genesis of conviction." *What proves what* was a difficult subject even before psycho-history was invented, and the query is particularly troublesome in biography, where the vividness of a report or the repetition of an act may give a totally false impression of motive and character.

That is why the criminal law carefully excludes certain references to character and is content to proceed without proof of motive. Consult experienced judges and trial lawyers and this is what you are likely to be

*A tendency parallel to the psycho-historian's mixing of the orders of evidence is the drive to make psychiatric opinion prevail over legal methods in ascertaining the guilt of the accused. The objections to this movement rest on the historian's view of evidence and include the charge that "psychiatric diagnoses are virtually irreversible: the initial diagnostic criteria are vague anyway . . . [and] a certain reluctance to admit error is characteristic of people and institutions generally" (Ulric Neisser, *Science* 180 [June 15, 1973]: 1116).

told: "It is always dangerous to impute motives to any man in regard to anything he says or does."[7] And again: "No doubt there is a motive behind all our actions, and few if any sane persons act without a reason. It would be wrong, however, to assume that the reason can always be appreciated by another person."[8] After such exemplary caution on the part of men who have studied and questioned hundreds of people under revealing conditions of stress, our paper-bred biographers and psychologists look immature and brash: *they* know the motives and can supply them in any desired jargon.

Freud's famous "Leonardo" essay is often cited in contrast, as a model of what psychoanalytic interpretation can bring out that nobody else had seen. But to the mind nurtured on evidence what Freud brings out seems slight as well as doubtful: (1) that Leonardo was a homosexual because his father abandoned him to his mother and thus fostered a one-sided relationship. (But the father's abandonment has been disputed and one diagnostic incident has been shown false, owing to a mistranslation of the key Italian word.) And (2) that Leonardo's habits as an artist—e.g., not finishing work begun—derive from this now disputed sexual development. Here determinism breaks down at the first contrary instance, say, Goethe, who also found finishing difficult, though he grew up with two parents and was an energetic heterosexual.*

The demurrer to analytic evidence is not due, as some like to think, to the ignorance or neurotic resistance of the critical historian, but to his acute sense of

*In other writings, Freud's analyses of art and artists are distressingly jejune, though he was himself a sensitive judge of art. His magnificent essay on Dostoevsky is convincing for several reasons, one of them being that the novelist's treatment of his characters is close to Freud's mode of thought. On the "Leonardo," see Henry F. Ellenberger, *The Discovery of the Unconscious* (New York, 1970), pp. 530–31.

how complex the makeup of an event—and much more that of a great personality—invariably is. This fundamental perception is linked with his professional view of cause and condition to be discussed in chapter 5. Here it suffices to quote Freud again in a situation where his candor supports the present argument: "I once allowed myself to reproach a true and worthy friend for no other reason than certain manifestations which I interpreted from his unconscious activity. He took it amiss and wrote me a letter in which he bade me not to treat my friends by psychoanalysis. I had to admit that he was right and I appeased him with my answer."[9] If an observable, intimately known living being is to be exempt from an analysis that is not genuinely clinical, what is to be said of essaying it upon the unobservable, never-encountered dead?

In an engaging article, "On the Nature of Psycho-Historical Evidence," which uses Gandhi's autobiography as illustrative material, Mr. Erikson tries nevertheless to establish parity between the clinician and the historian: "selected portions of the past impose themselves on our renewed awareness and claim continued actuality."[10] But this echo of Collingwood's idea of history can serve the parallel only in the most general, abstract way. The historian's "portions of the past" speak mostly in words that anybody can consult, and the story they tell—as Collingwood put it—re-enacts itself easily in the living imagination; whereas the clinician's portions of the past "impose themselves" only as symptoms in a mass of irrelevancies. To make us "re-enact" this other story the analyst must piece together elaborately and interpret heavily. Not all interpreters find the same signs or read them the same way; theirs is a study in detection such as historians indulge in when their material is at its thinnest—using, say, hints and allusions in a text to establish a date; "great event" must mean the defeat of the Armada, *therefore* soon after 1588. It is an engrossing pastime, but nobody dares put much weight on the resulting structure. It does not satisfy the demand for *evidence,* a term in which we should always feel the vividness of: "it is *evident* that . . ." Accordingly one must conclude with regret that Mr. Erikson's essay—perhaps the best authorized to make a case for psycho-history—does not deal with evidence at all. Its subject is semeiology, the theory of signs and symptoms.*

Among signs, moreover, the inveterate historical mind is particularly wary of accepting the startling little cause, the tiny detail that speaks volumes. Curiosity is sometimes the love of unmasking, and biographical research a disguised form of scandal-mongering. It was this foible that Lytton Strachey exploited in his lives of *Eminent Victorians* and subsequent works. He believed his portraits would seem searching if he took as tell-tale signs something not only small but mean.† The isolated, equivocal, unsuspected fact stimulates the fantasy and the habit of pseudo-reasoning, the kind of putting two and two together necessary for reading mystery novels or being a successful gossip. Thoreau gave an amusing instance of the pastime when he said that finding a trout in the milk was circumstantial evidence of the strongest sort, though in fact the number of possibilities to be excluded by inquiry before deliberate dilution could be proved is considerable. Still, the small point sticks; it is remembered as the trait that

*It is surprising how often in somatic medicine itself symptoms recorded in the past lead to divergent conclusions or to none. The plague of Athens has never been identified. The malformation of Byron's leg (as one will find at the cost of much fruitless research) has not received an accepted diagnosis, in spite of drawings presumably made at the time. Physicians still dispute as to clubfoot or polio and are not even agreed as to which leg the bad one was!

†His quite adolescent estimate of Disraeli, for example, shows how the penchant becomes an intellectual vice. Victoria's reign turns into make-believe with a Disraeli who is a figure of fun, judged by his youthful curls and his elderly love letters.

made the individual "come to life" and only an historian or wise judge of the world knows enough to fight against the false verdict.*

Sound historians go even beyond the refusal to trust the meaning of small points. They avoid stressing certain large traits for which the evidence is plentiful, lest the proportions of the figure be distorted in the reader's too impressionable mind. Plutarch knew of this danger and Harold Nicolson remarked on it when he said that in writing of Curzon he played down his miserly habits and ungovernable temper, for fear nobody should remember anything else about him.† This restraint is important, because emotion enters into understanding. The reader feels at every moment, even when he believes that he is only absorbing information. Therefore the writer whose tone is knowing or technical or cleverly inferential will persuade many readers that his very manner is evidence.§ When interlarded with solid bits of history, this purely cosmetic evidence appears to guarantee "depth" and superior truth.

What Are Figures Evidence Of?

It is customary to say that the most effective lie is the statistical lie, and—because the dictum is a commonplace—not to believe it. But when the historian demurs on principle at the evidential value of figures, he is not thinking of fraudulent or slovenly statistics. Bad exam-

*Chesterton treats this question with his usual good sense: "It is the snare and sin of biographers that they tend to see significance in everything; characteristic carelessness if their hero drops his pipe, and characteristic carefulness if he picks it up again" (G. K. Chesterton, *Robert Browning* [New York, 1905], p. 5).

†Plutarch's excellent maxim is: ". . . without swerving from the truth . . . neither wholly leave out, nor yet too pointedly express what is defective" (apropos of Lucullus, in the life of Cimon).

§"He was one of the horrid creatures who write with a wink at you, which sets the wicked part of us on fire, . . . who leads you up to the curtain and agitates it, and bids you retire on tiptoe" (George Meredith, *The Amazing Marriage* [London, 1902], p. 3).

ples prove nothing but their own worthlessness. The skeptic about quanto-history takes a different ground altogether. He is mindful, to start with, of the difficulties of method mentioned earlier. But great as these are, they seem to him dwarfed by the difficulty of stating what counts and measurements make evident—"give a sight of."

This imagining or imaging of past reality is the point of history: the evident supplies the historian with images to communicate. It would be interesting, if it were possible, to test the viewer of tables and graphs after his scrutiny and find out what images were formed and remained in *his* mind's eye. First, no doubt, some abstract shapes—ratios of large and small, correlations of time and quantity, curves of gradualness or angles of mutation or slopes of rise and fall, and so on. There is value for history in these perceptions, since they are as much part of the common mode of thought as cause-and-effect or before-and-after. But studies exclusively based on such modes seem better designed for reference than for comprehension. In any direct observation of life or any reading of history, the quality of the quantity and their joint meaning all come in one cluster, and the succession of scenes is felt and remembered almost without effort. Numbers lack this precision. Consider: yesterday's big parade may be three times as numerous as the small one of last week, but if it is made up of uncostumed stragglers and lacks music, it is not nearly so impressive. If moreover the march has not actually been seen but its size has been measured by the length of time it took to pass a certain point, the evidence as to anything other than that fact is virtually nil. Figures of this sort may be convenient for comparing the relative traffic obstruction caused by parades throughout the year, but they leave out everything that one needs in order to judge importance or recapture the impression of reality.

If this example is thought too obvious, consider the

sort of evidence that figures are often thought to provide—the influence of a book, measured by the number of copies or editions sold. Some historians accept the connection, but others trust their live experience rather than the figures. They know at first hand that there is no proportion between the circulation of a book and its influence. Toynbee's *Study of History* was a best-seller without influence. Montesquieu and Marx were scarcely read in their original form and their thought changed the world. Rousseau was widely read and correspondingly powerful: you never can tell —until you look into it with your own eyes.* A future archeologist who should find the Housing Bureau list of buildings in Greater New York would not know that the dominant form of architecture was the skyscraper. Numbers would tell him the opposite. To state the matter broadly, the "dominance" of a certain number or point on a graph over another may differ radically from the social or cultural dominance of an idea, a feeling, or an artifact.

Again, in the effort to show by numbers a uniformity between past and present, the distribution of essential features is often overlooked. Of recent years "evidence" has several times been adduced to show that from the Civil War to the end of the century the proportion of drug addicts in the United States was as great as it is now. How this is reliably known can be questioned, but numerical validity matters less even than the unhistorical outlook which can entertain the idea of a likeness between the two groups of drug-takers: from 1865 to 1900 their hobby did not arouse worldwide alarm and repressive measures; they did not add to crime on the streets; their weakness was not the basis of a billion-dollar traffic reaching down into the lower schools and punctuated by gang warfare and Supreme

*"Every year there is at least one major best-seller which almost everybody buys and almost nobody reads" (Robert A. Carter, *Authors Guild Bulletin*, October/December 1973).

Court decisions; nor did their plight inspire legislation, research, the setting up of clinics, and a vast contentious and inconclusive literature, scientific, novelistic, and theatrical.

Generality, Actuality, Objectivity

The obsessive monism which affirms that whatever exists can be measured achieves its goal by taking the historical evidence and denaturing it into a featureless product. As in Mercator's projection map, the earth is flattened out on a piece of paper and marked off in squares. The device is useful for navigation; it can only mislead where the sole aim is to reconstruct reality. That is why the historian who has not lost the sense of the actual—the sense that led him to history in the first place—doubts the numerical.

When "violence" is hypostatized into a thing, the historian wants to know the circumstances of each violent incident: was this one maliciously reported to the prefect as political when it was only a drunken brawl? Did the local authorities, for their own reasons, exaggerate the number? Doesn't this report come from a government-subsidized newspaper? Did slovenly bureaucratic methods count some incidents twice? The quanto-historian was doubtless aware of these diversities and sifted out the comparable, but in the statistics that are produced with much labor and read with little pleasure, the leap from evidence to tabulation comes early and is not the difficult feat that it ought to be. The upshot, when certain studies achieve credence and fame, is that two or three generations live under the sway of "scientific" findings destined for overthrow by the same statistical means.

It is not the purpose of this book to teach the canons of evidence or the principles by which history may be written and trusted.* There are numerous views of the

*On such matters, see Checklist, no. 30.

nature of history, and their differences do not affect the present critique. But its bearing requires that something be said about objectivity. Numbers have the reputation of being objective because their mutual relations are at nobody's mercy; they seem to form a closed society under tyrannical rule. Psychology, if mathematical, partakes of this absolute and the depth psychology founded by Freud claims an equally scientific validity.

Against these rigid things, amenable to systematic handling, the historian reaffirms the merit of his type of evidence. It consists of what biased and fallible men have written, plus relics and records of neutral but indicative meaning. On this elastic base, the historian nevertheless pretends to objectivity. Professor Langer himself, when on his "old" assignment as a distinguished diplomatic historian, summons the government to release official documents sooner and more fully than it has done, so that "scholars who are professionally committed to the writing of objective history" can enlighten the people about what happened at critical moments in their recent history.[11]

But surely, says the psycho- or quanto-historian, our old-fashioned forebears' old-fashioned "commitment" is not enough. In selecting, assembling, and interpreting the documents, subjectivity reigns. That is true; so true, that the methodic historians themselves cannot escape the limitation. They go to the common hoard of facts and choose, assemble, and interpret. Mr. Erikson acknowledges this weakness—if it is one—when he calls the therapeutic encounter (which he equates with historical research) "disciplined subjectivity."[12]* And

*In genuine historians the disciplining of subjectivity is a second nature that is proof against temptations. In his account of the discovery and interpretation of *The Secret Gospel* (1973), Professor Morton Smith says of his colleague Professor Nock: "His philological knowledge was vast, his judgment impeccable, and his objectivity such that, in spite of his prejudice against Clementine authorship, he often pointed out evidence that went to confirm it" (p. 27).

the quantifier might as well accept the phrase for himself, since he too picks out and classifies by intuition the same scattered pieces of evidence.

At bottom, then, there is no difference among them. None possesses a more secure base than the others. Thought can only start from an immediate and convincing perception; all evidence rests on the feeling that something is plainly so as soon as apprehended—for instance, that the sentence you are now reading begins with the words: "all evidence rests . . ." No one can go behind your perception or ask for proof of its rightness; nor would a mistake in the reading change the nature of the act of cognition when correctly performed.

Doubt and difficulty enter when the evidence, good or bad in itself, is taken up and handled. That is the point where the historian claims for his handling an intellectual merit denied to his improvers: he does not translate the evidence into a language foreign to the data—numbers or symptomatography. He thereby leaves his "disciplined subjectivity" open to scrutiny and amendment. "Translated evidence," on the contrary, generates a special form of error, over and above common bias and blunder. The psycho-historian's diagnosis, owing to its tenuous hold on meager signs, tends (as was said) to be doctrinaire and irreversible. As for the quanto-historian's figures, they are, owing to their laborious production, rarely subject to a recount. Other workers take up new samples for study and simply *overlie* the first. And somewhere all these findings petrify into "facts." The inner check in any historian, plain or "scientific," is intellectual honesty, but the one *external* discipline for the subjectivity that all share is evidence accessible to others.

4

The Question of Motive

The Double Aspect of Intention

In speaking of an historian's motive for writing history, one must distinguish between his purpose and his motive properly so-called—what moves him to study and write, as compared with what he hopes to show or to supply. The primary purpose of much of the new history is Explanation; the ulterior motive is Action.*

The type of explanation sought is the scientific; that is, showing a connection ("durable link") between the facts and a definable cause. Classification, then analysis, then prediction is the sequence that leads naturally to action. In the two books on slavery cited earlier, the authors admit—indeed proclaim—the wish to answer pressing questions. It is a high-minded wish, and in those instances fastidious and self-critical as well. But it is not unfair to call the attempt a manipulating of the past in hopes of manipulating the future: if we can relate the slaveholder's mind via the ethos of the concentration camp to determinants in infancy (or, alternatively, in society) we may be able to abolish the evils of slavery in all its forms.† The goal is to find mechanisms: the word recurs.

*This motive, needless to say, does not act by itself. It is singled out here from the mixture of personal motives because of its functional relation to the primary purpose and because of its public avowal by "committed" scholars.

†But see above, pp. 36–37, a few of the incommensurable types of slavery.

Before going into the prerequisites of making history a science, one should take a look at the restless desire itself, which has been haunting History for so many generations. The French "Fatalists" of the 1830s and 40s, Buckle, Marx, Tolstoy, the latter-day Positivists, the post-Darwinian historical schools at the close of the last century, the "new" historians summoned in the next by Lamprecht—all wanted a science of history and some thought they had found the way to it. What is their common characteristic? The longing for certitude, which some hoped to find by reaching down to a substratum, a rock-bottom element from which everything in history could be seen to spring. Marx's choice of bottom is well known. Others chose climate or geography or race or the dominant form of intellect. Durkheim, divorcing from history, relied on "social fact," a fundamental reality independent of human psychology and ascertainable only by statistics.*

The common effort, in other words, was to get rid of the human mind and will. It still is. Our contemporary psycho-historian, by an unwitting play on words, flatters himself that *depth* psychology points to a realm from which comes, by the social interaction of unconsciouses, the crazy quilt of history. Those of the new historians who are drawn by anthropology make culture the conditioner, a modified version of determinism by race or intellectual forms. The great point is: to describe the mechanism. From mechanisms will be deduced formulas with which to direct action. That the hope of directing action is inconsistent with an unconscious or collective determinism is never an obstacle to the creators of social science.

*Durkheim's influence on the educated public was very great. In 1903 Anatole France predicted that in Utopia history would be replaced by statistics (*Sur la Pierre blanche*). Renan's *Future of Science* (1890, unpublished since 1848) chimed in with the current conviction that literature and the arts and humanities were clumsy approximations that would soon be perfected by science and as sciences.

More important than consistency is the character of the formulas which are to be the passport to understanding. The thought-cliché natural to an age of physical science is that what is most fundamental, most *underlying,* is automatically most enlightening. This is an unexamined impression. Chemical molecules and the particles of physics lie deeper than the Id; so the psycho-historian should push on to a chemo-history and a nuclear biography. The suggestion is not logic turning into fantasy. The branch of psychology known as psycho-acoustics has made amazing progress in reducing perception (sensory phenomena) to equivalence with energy fluctuations in the stimulus. According to Professor McGill, "The net outcome is that the listener can be painted out of the picture in the ideal way that sensory psychologists strive to discover." The achievement consists in having shown that "a mathematically ideal observer and a simple energy detector, although worlds apart conceptually, behave rather alike."[1] It follows that the "ideal way" to arrive at formulas for understanding the mechanism of human events is to accept mathematical models as the equivalents of man and society. These can then be permanently "painted out of the picture."

What Answers Are Required?

Such a reductio ad absurdum compels one to tackle a problem as difficult as it is neglected, neglected perhaps because it seems to be no problem at all: what *is* explanation? At what point do we "understand"? How do we know that we do?* Again by analogy with

*Little has been written on Explanation except by logicians and philosophers of science, who are alike concerned with the validity of inference, induction, and deduction. They take for granted the feeling and the *satisfyingness* of explanation. See the three papers "On the Anatomy of Explanation" by Arthur W. Ghent in *Bios* 33 (2 and 3) and 34 (1) (1962–63).

science, it is taken as a matter of course that we can never know too much about a subject and that every fresh statement "adds to our understanding." The authors of *History as Social Science* mention but do not settle this great question: "The transfer from other disciplines of insights often derived from the study of different subjects . . . entails obvious hazards. . . . Yet it is the kind of risk that the conscientious historian . . . is well equipped to take. This is not to say that these conceptual imports will make possible a history any more definitive than what has gone before. They open up new kinds and levels of understanding, and there will be other kinds and levels to follow."[2] We face another metaphor: what *are* these "kinds" and "levels"?

Explanation is not an absolute term, any more than understanding is an experience capable of being fitted into a box. Explanation can be, as in science, downward, by the discovery and enumeration of simpler elements—the Cartesian method. For example, if we want to know why an incandescent bulb gives light by electricity, we go "down" step by step to the system of particles in the glowing material and find out why their motions, well-known under many conditions, cannot help producing light under *these* conditions. We stop there, resting in the fact that things are so and not otherwise.

In history the prevailing mode of explanation is not downward but outward—on the same plane as that of the question asked. If we ask why Napoleon was so swift and sure in the execution of his plans, we do not say: because he ate a given amount of protein daily and his brain was of such and such a cubic capacity. Food and brain were certainly indispensable conditions of his activity, but they do not interest us; we take them for granted. We look rather to the contents of his training at Brienne, his ability to take the measure of men and events, his handling of rivals and opponents, and his acquired technique for moving armies and minds in obedience to his will. We confirm our judgment by observing that whenever he neglected part of his usual program, because of other duties or because of prejudice, he failed. We then believe we understand him better than before, even though we have stayed on one level of observation and reflection.

To change levels and explore portions of his being in which he resembled thousands of his contemporaries—liability to disease, imputed neurosis, bad temper, sexual tastes—would not be to understand *him,* though items under those headings might provide picturesque trimmings to a portrait. It is clear that if such details were piled on to excess they would swamp understanding altogether. Napoleon would disappear under a mass of trivialities giving the impression that he was the most commonplace of men: he combed his hair thus, he grew fat around the waist, etc., etc. A demand for explanation can be flouted by the sort of answer given to it.

Explanation and Diagnosis: The Difference

But suppose—and this is the psycho-historian's claim—that these same details change from commonplace to significant when viewed in the special light of psychoanalysis. Would not the "pattern" disclosed "add to our understanding," deepen our explanation? The likelihood is that the analysis would not explain so much as pave the way for action: it would "diagnose the trouble." Understanding in human affairs means imagining, visualizing, reliving, and above all *individualizing,* not reducing to type and kind, as diagnosis is meant to do.

It is true that historical explanation often consists in

showing likeness between the unknown and the familiar. But unless such similarities are used solely to facilitate description, the device is bound to be reductive and misleading. One form of this error is the genetic fallacy, which "explains" an event or condition by reference to its simpler antecedents: the oak is nothing but an acorn with a little sun and water added. A diagnosis or other technical explanation is a statement of this sort—and legitimately so, since it is meant to save thinking, to guide the analyst on his course, by delivering to him in short form all the previous work that led to the framing of concepts, symptoms, and mechanisms.

If, as will appear more fully later, it is not only the nature but also the duty of History to move in the opposite direction from diagnosis, typology, and technical analysis, then Explanation in History is properly defined by the demands of the common reader. His "understanding" in both senses—that is, his intellect and what satisfies it—is governed by a far subtler use of words than the technical. The signs and intimations to which he responds are more numerous and more free. There is no reason why he should have to go into training before taking up a history. His curiosity about the past should not condemn him to a siege of *hineinstudiren* before a particular doctrine, much less to weighing pros and cons among the dubieties and contradictions of rival systems. He wants to read and learn. His feeling that something has been explained derives entirely from what William James called "the sentiment of rationality," the impression that familiar and unfamiliar elements have been put into intelligible relation by someone who gives tokens of trustworthiness. That is intelligible which he finds sufficiently congruent with his experience (direct or vicarious) to make him accept the neighboring strangeness and integrate it into a new and enlarged view of the facts. And for this purpose, the explanatory virtue of common speech cannot be surpassed.

Understanding an Unfortunate Young Man

What has just been said can be tested by a short biographical example, drawn from English life in the seventeenth century.

> Charles Mohun,* born in 1674 of noble parents (his mother was herself the daughter of the Earl of Anglesey, while his father was the third of his line) was conceived under a baleful star, and violence was in his blood. While the child was still only a year old the father, a gallant and a blade in the very "best" tradition, was killed while seconding the Earl of Cavendish in a duel with Lord Power. . . .
>
> The widowed Baroness, inconsolable in his loss, turned all her love upon her baby son and with steady, insistent spoiling prepared him surely for the same bloody end that had destroyed his father. But that was far in the future. Meantime the lad grew from a precocious child, surrounded constantly by obedient women, into an imperious, dominating youth. Handsome, charming when need be; forthright and frank in speech and manner, almost ungovernable when thwarted; suffocating under the artificial petticoat life around him—and rich.
>
> This combination of frustration and wealth has been disastrous to better men than Mohun, both before his time and since, but with him it was to prove fatal. Growing personal unfulfilment, the glamorous example of his swaggering father, the cloying affection of his mother and above all the awareness that

*Pronounced "Moon."

> Life was there for the mere taking—all these things simmered and smouldered inside him.
>
> Yet there was much in him that was good —perhaps only a certain moral strength was lacking. He was the friend of anyone who wanted his friendship. He was a good listener to the troubles of others, and a ready sympathiser. In the physical sense he was fearless. Above all, he was utterly loyal both to his friends and their causes. And it is ironical, but true, that his good qualities led him more into disaster than his bad ones ever did. For as a result, perhaps, of his stifled upbringing on the family estates in Devon he possessed an inexhaustible capacity for picking worthless friends.
>
> . . .
>
> He soon found himself in bad company. Captain Richard Hill of the Dragoons, rising thirty, cynical, fashionable and tough, noted ruffler and cut-throat, had but two passions in life; horses and women. Horses, he not only loved but respected; women —easier to come by than the thorough-bred and cheaper to keep—he loved in endless procession and despised accordingly. It made him irresistible, of course. Mohun became devoted to him.[3]

The upshot of this friendship was an early and ignoble death for Mohun, after two trials for murder before the House of Lords.*

Now the test of the biographer's explanatory powers is this: let anyone with some experience of life ask himself whether he understands Lord Mohun's character. The question is not, Can the writer "account for it"? in the sense of why it had to be so and not otherwise; but rather, Does the description given make us visualize,

*See Thackeray's *Henry Esmond* for the duel in which Mohun and the Duke of Hamilton both perished (bk. III, chap. V).

sympathize, regret? Surely that is how we understand our family and friends. We reflect and compare; we remember young men rather like Lord Mohun, ruined by fatherless, matriarchal influence. We remember besides—this is most important—other boys reared by doting mothers and aunts who did *not* turn out dauntless and depraved but, possibly, timid and straitlaced. There are infinite varieties of character *and circumstance*.*

This direct demonstration of what understanding is needs no other support: you understand Mohun or you do not. But in fairness to the psycho-portraitist we may imagine the supplement he proposes to give. He might say that Mohun's recklessness was overcompensation for a girlish, overprotected childhood; or that, oedipally in love with his mother, he was acting—and overacting—the father role; or even that his known "loyalty" to young men friends was unconscious homosexuality, balanced (and also symbolized) by impulsive swordplay. There are no doubt other and better psychological observations that a competent analyst (whose words are here simulated without authority) might make. But what would they explain—not about the workings of the unconscious, but about Charles Mohun—that we do not already know?

Take a parallel case that has been dealt with psychohistorically. Rutherford B. Hayes was reared and oversheltered by his mother, his sister, and a maiden cousin-aunt. His biographer, Mr. Harry Barnard, says of him: "Neighbors . . . considered him as 'timid as a girl.' " Later "other influences . . . set up in him a defensive, countering trend toward manliness." After ac-

*Mohun's first murder was willful, but accidental in the sense that the timing of unrelated events permitted his brashness to take effect—circumstance. Another imaginable youth, of the same psychic makeup but apprenticed to a tailor, would probably not have known how to wield a sword: circumstance again.

tion in the Civil War, Hayes became a strong, self-confident person: "he had become," says Mr. Barnard somewhat curiously, "his own father symbol."[4] From this set of facts we may infer that early modes of behavior, of conscious or unconscious origin, are modifiable, that character traits do change, which heightens the danger of substituting a fixed diagnostic formula for what should be a progressive series of descriptions. An explanation by childhood determinants leaves no room for one of the most easily observed facts, the *development* of character. In other words, diagnosis is more likely to close and restrict the imagination than to open and enlarge it.*

Cause and Condition

Against these weighty considerations the psychohistorian has one more argument of principle: even granting that diagnosis does not enrich the historical imagination, doesn't the historian want to know the causes of things? This pertinent question could easily start a discussion of the tangled issue of causation in human affairs, in natural science, and in historiography. But a full treatment would divert the present essay from its object, which is to find out and compare the intentions of two types of scholarship which some are bent on reducing to one.

*This conclusion must not be taken to rule out special studies (diagnostic if appropriate) of an individual or a group whose history demands the specialty: we need a physician to tell us about scurvy in the British navy of the eighteenth century and other specialists to deal with such topics as are listed in the concluding chapter. The historian is always happy to find such studies, e.g., Dr. Edwin A. Weinstein's account of Woodrow Wilson's neurological troubles, dating back to 1896. The article is based on medical records and does not impose a medical explanation upon other than medical events. Rather, it relates history and disease in masterly fashion, a model of the special study (*Journal of American History* 57 [September 1970]: 324–51).

On the subject of causation the historian is a philosophical pragmatist; he ascertains the conditions relevant to the situation or event and gives an account of those best able to produce understanding. A single cause linked to a single effect is not an historical but a laboratory possibility. The difference between them is that life presents a multiplicity of conditions, all of which are causes, whereas laboratory technique permits the artificial isolation and control of single conditions in a one-to-one relation within a closed system.

In an historical situation, dozens of conditions are of no interest, because obvious or constant or merely curious or undiscoverable. In the Defenestration of Prague, for example, one of the conditions for the fall of the two men thrown out of the window was gravitation—we take it for granted. One of the conditions of the envoys' survival was the presence of mulch in the moat where they fell, and this may be mentioned, to exclude miracle and mystery. But the bodies' precise angle of impact and the muscle tone in each that prevented serious injury are neither ascertainable nor of concern to any reader.*

When, therefore, the psycho-historian proposes to give *a* cause for Hitler's actions (a syndrome or complex does not change the oneness of the suggestion), he assumes that he has proved a correlation of cause and effect just as if he were a laboratory scientist working

*In his chapter on Causation, John Stuart Mill makes the point with his usual exhaustiveness, though without reference to the historian's interest. One of Mill's illustrations will none the less delight the biographer: "Though we call prussic acid the agent of a person's death, the whole of the vital and organic properties of the patient are as actively instrumental as the poison, in the chain of effects which so rapidly terminates his sentient existence" (*A System of Logic* [New York, 1881], bk. III, chap. V, pp. 242–43).

Similarly, the law holds that except in certain enumerated cases a person is deemed to have committed homicide although his act is not the immediate or not the sole cause of death. See J. F. Stephen, *Digest of the Criminal Law*, 5th ed. (London, 1894), p. 178.

within a closed system. At that point the historian objects with a set of questions that were neatly grouped by the late Herbert Feis at the conference previously cited: "How adequate psychological knowledge is, how stable it is, how precise it is, and how agreed it is." As to stability, judges apparently differ. The theorists of psycho-history invoke Freud and speak of psychoanalysis or of dynamic psychiatry as if those names covered unified teachings. Yet a slight acquaintance with the literature is enough to show that radical conflicts subsist. There is even a school of "existential" analysts, who maintain that the neurotic is aware of the role he is playing and the mask he uses to misrepresent his inner battle. "Unconscious" thereby means not quite what it says.

Again, in the interesting works of Dr. Thomas Szasz, the classic relation of patient to analyst is disallowed and the very notion of mental illness put out of court.[5] The rifts began with the first great disciples of Freud, and the bulk of ensuing theory and controversy shows how arbitrary and ambiguous must be the use of psychoanalytic formulas in nontechnical literature. Psycho-historians rarely keep the "conceptual frameworks" of the several schools as distinct as they are in the pages of Professor Elkins. Yet without strictness of method and meaning, what is there to compel belief? This laxness would seem to go to Mr. Feis's point about precision.

And as to adequacy one must point out that analytic thought has established itself as cogent, not by being generally "agreed" in the academies of pure science, but by the popular diffusion of its terms. Certain ideas have come to be readily understood by the public, regardless of their doctrinal origins or exact meaning. This dilution is what overtakes all great bodies of thought. The words *complex, introvert, extrovert, ambivalence, fixation, repression, guilt, anxiety, ego, id, superego, projection, oedipal, hysterical, father-figure, accident-prone, narcissism, inferiority, manic-depressive, death wish, wish-fulfillment, paranoid, schizophrenic,* and some others less hackneyed occur in ordinary conversation and mark a spot in the mental geography of the speakers. The terms come from Charcot, Freud, Jung, Adler, and their disciples indifferently, and they manage to remain clear without being exact or consistent. Thus when Mr. Barnard, speaking of Rutherford Hayes, refers to "the fixations in which Fanny [his sister] and Sardis [his uncle] were the chief figures," we readily understand that by "fixations" he means "deep attachments." For we see that these emotional relations were of different intensities: Hayes experienced no tension or pain or any reluctance to marry on account of his uncle as he did on account of his sister. The very plural "fixations" indicates that the word is being used without technical significance.

We are far, then, from the scientific rigor that would lead us to accept any of the current diagnoses of men and history as supplying causes. Paradoxically, it is owing to the very principle of depth psychology that it cannot supply them, for individuals may be regarded either as differing radically—what we mean by unique—or as fundamentally the same. If unique, then the "factors" dredged up from below and linked to infantile careers—the dominant mother, copulating parents, sadistic sibling—have nothing distinctive to tell us. They apply uniformly wherever found: that is the definition of a cause. But if individuals are seen as substantially the same there is no point to analyzing one more than another, therapy excepted. That is why in history all that the analytic effort achieves by substituting the "cause" for the event is to lessen our feeling of reality about the details we start with. Chain-smoking may well express a regressive desire to suck the breast, but sucking the breast does not lead to lung cancer, and our hero's death still has to be explained by chain-smoking.*

Words and Explanation

By way of compensation, the depth psychologists—and Freud more than all the rest—have contributed to the historian something he can no longer do without: the words and ideas referred to a moment ago as popularized during the last hundred years. It is no accident that psychoanalysis is the one psychology favored by the present medicators of history: though theirs is not the only school to have advanced the study of the mind in our time, their vocabulary is the only post-classical one that has gained currency.† And this success through common speech illustrates a principle: in order to be of use to the historian, psychological as well as other technical terms must first fall into the public domain. It has always been so. In the sketch about young Mohun, the writer says he was "conceived under a baleful star and violence was in his blood." Here judicial astrology and an early genetic psychology are combined through terms now in common speech, the reader's native and only idiom.

Must we then, asked a scoffer at the conference, take our psychoanalytic terms from the butcher and the

*This argument applies mutatis mutandis to all linear determinisms. Consumption and syphilis do not cause the artistic atmosphere of certain works of genius, nor do the earthquakes along the San Andreas fault cause the breakup of those marriages that do in fact break up after the earth-shaking experience. See J. J. Fried, *Life along the San Andreas Fault* (New York, 1973).

†For many reasons, the classic of psychology most useful to the historian and biographer is William James's *Principles of Psychology*, 2 vols. (1890). His concreteness, breadth of reference, esthetic perception, historical knowledge, and unfailing sense of complexity make him endlessly suggestive. As present-day psychologists have remarked, he defies obsolescence, particularly on such topics as belief, will, attention, and the stream of consciousness.

baker? To which the answer of any reader of the great historians is: yes. It is they—bakers, butchers, and historians—who set the standard. Barring an occasional need to employ the jargon of a trade or profession (shipping, war, coinage), the historian uses no language but that which will bring his narrative within the literate man's capacity to follow.

It can of course be argued that if psychological terms are not to be used with technical precision, they might as well be omitted altogether—why "fixations" when we can say "deep attachments"? Much is to be said for simplicity, yet a writer is entitled to any words he thinks will convey his meaning, and those chosen are bound to vary with the times. Our civilization puts a premium on words suggestive of science. Where an earlier psychology spoke of "conviction of sin," "state of orison," or "counter-conversion," we speak of anxiety, projection, counter-transference, and the like, without on that account denying ourselves the nomenclature of astrology, the four humors, and the Marxist names for approved or sinful attitudes. These phrases we mix are not, of course, equivalents; they are only signposts within different mappings of the mind, and alike subject to uncertainty, argument, and misuse. Their utility depends on having shed the pretense of exclusiveness and exactitude.*

Numbers and Explanation

For the student dissatisfied with plain history, and doubtful of psychology, another path to understanding is that which the quanto-historian believes he is fol-

*"The chief use of psychology (apart from curing people, if it does) seems to me to be to restate old truths in modern jargon which people can understand; and if psychology helps people towards truth which they cannot apprehend when put in simple theological language, so much the better" (T. S. Eliot, "A Commentary," *Criterion*, April 1932, p. 472).

lowing: induction on a broad scale. Its effort is to overcome hasty conclusions, mere impressions, old prejudices, and conventional knowledge. The records of day-to-day life in such repositories as police archives and town halls seem to promise more breadth and truth than are afforded by documents consciously composed for posterity and full of explicit or implicit conclusions. The aim is to attain generality, to establish a trend. If a relation of cause and effect imposes itself on the mind as the work of tabulation goes on, it quantifies itself on paper in the same process. The table or graph is bound to give more assured understanding than any listing of conditions and estimate of their force, couched in the historian's vague qualifying words.

Some who object to explanation by number argue that human affairs lack the regularity shown by events in physics and therefore cannot be studied in a comparable way. The argument is misplaced. There are regularities in human life; there is regularity in human character. The very existence of society depends on those regularities, established by convention or interest and enforced by will or desire. The moment one says "a law-abiding citizen," one implies a regularity in relation to a well-defined set of acts, namely crimes, and the extent of that regularity would not be hard to calculate; a simple subtraction and multiplication would suffice—assuming that crime statistics were well kept.

But regularities of this sort are precisely the ones that need no study. They are taken for granted by the historian, whether or not he is a quantifier. It is the irregularities that arouse curiosity and—in the quanto-historian—his desire to tame them by showing that *underneath* there are governing *regulas,* rules. It is there that he mistakes the character of his material, as well as the nature of his own procedure.

First of all, statistics have to do only with effects; they

say nothing about causes or motives. Divorces, suicides, misdirected letters are effects which, however regular in number within any nation or period, do not lead back to a uniform source. By the same token, these effects are not fated, binding upon any group or individual. The rate or incidence may change suddenly; there are no laws "governing" the behavior of a people or person in these or any other respects. As everybody knows who understands probability, the odds remain the same at every throw of the dice, even if a run of double sixes has struck the imagination of the players as precluding yet one more. In situations where, unlike divorce or suicide or dice-throwing, the usual regularities are thrown into confusion—for example, in a state of martial law—probability itself is silent. As Shaw said, perhaps foreseeing the quanto-historian: "Chaos has no statistics; it has only statisticians."[6]

Meeting the Criteria of Science

The illicit move from unified statistics to diversified cause is not the only defect of would-be scientific history. Two indispensable conditions have to be met before a durable link between an effect and a cause can be asserted. One is prediction; the other is the exclusion of different hypotheses. It is not enough for the inquirer to say: "here is a recurrent connection between *a* and *b*. I have come across no evidence that goes counter to it." He must be able to say further: "the evidence for my hypothesis by its character excludes rival suppositions." This is required because in logic simple induction from classified instances stands on very shaky ground. Even after recording innumerable black crows, the possibility remains of finding a white one. The durable link of bird and color is therefore unproved.

But when a hypothesis permits the observer to predict and the event confirms his prediction, then the durability of the connection is enormously strengthened; for the known structure of experience makes it unlikely that an altogether different correlation would lead to the same foreseeable results in the same measured amounts. Why numbers seem to jibe with the interconnections of the physical world is a puzzle but they do.* And that is why to talk of scientific formulas when numbers are not involved is to indulge in metaphor. The substance of history, we know, is not amenable to measurement in the scientific sense; and prediction in history, though often validated, is not scientific prediction capable of sifting true explanations from false. An historian's forecast is an affair of worldly judgment such as everyone uses, more or less well, in the conduct of life. Tocqueville was sure that democracy would spread, and he was right. But for all the correctness of his prediction he could not chart the course or measure the strength of democratic tendencies, much less assert their permanence. Eighty-five years later, after the war that was to make the world safe for democracy, many observers predicted its further extension, only to be proved repeatedly wrong within the next few years.

Even supposing, contrary to fact, that quanto-history could carry out surveys so broad and so accurate that the regularities disclosed would permit truly mathematical statements of cause and effect, those statements would be so general as to afford no help of the kind desired. Long ago, James Fitzjames Stephen put the point with finality in an essay on the tenable meaning of "a science" of history: "Historical science would [like the law of gravitation] have no assignable relation to any particular state of facts. It would form a mere skeleton, giving nothing but hypothetical conclu-

*See E. P. Wigner, "The Unreasonable Effectiveness of Mathematics in the Natural Sciences," *Communications on Pure and Applied Mathematics* 13 (February 1960): 1–14.

sions, and always leaving unclassified a vast mass of circumstances which the historical philosopher would be able to consider in no other light than that of disturbing causes."[7]

The Motives behind the Purpose

The joint popularity of psycho- and quanto-history is not an accident—or a contradiction; for although nothing is more impalpable than the Id and more dense than town-hall records, they stand respectively for the individual and society, and the past of one or the other or both may well contain the influential secret about present and future. The two branches of the new history give an equal hold to the strong desire mentioned in an earlier connection: to solve pressing problems. No need, then, to continue treating the two separately: they have one endeavor.

The very phrase in which this endeavor is expressed is indicative of the will behind it. Other ages were beset by the difficulties of life; we call the same difficulties "problems," and thus imply that "solutions" exist.* The science-bred notion of the control of nature has reinforced the Enlightenment dream of remolding society, and the presence of huge, intricate, and unexampled problems in excessive numbers being by now an accepted belief, urgency is added to normal concern. Any intellectual effort that ignores present problems seems aloof and heartless and almost certainly trivial. Historical scholars tend to feel the moral burden in proportion to their youth, and they have good precedents for believing that history, like art, must "take part in the struggle": "Other historians tell us facts in

*Until about the turn of the nineteenth century the usual all-inclusive phrase was "the social question." Social problems (the term being influenced by the "problem play" which "resolved" them) came gradually into common use after 1875.

order to teach us facts. You do it in order to excite in the depths of our souls a strong indignation against mendacity, ignorance, hypocrisy, superstition, fanaticism, tyranny; and that indignation remains when the memory of facts is gone." Thus Diderot to Voltaire.[8] In the next century, Michelet at the outset of his work assigned himself the task of making history righteously blasphemous by mocking all false gods.

Under such obligations the work is once again subjected to a system or at least a doctrine, this time for reform or revolution.* The impulse is akin to that which produces wartime histories. Their quality, it is well known, is never very high, even when the author's mind is of high caliber, because the day's news is a distorting lens. A leading psycho-historian, Dr. Robert Jay Lifton, feeling the immediacy of war, has written the reverse of a patriotic work, but one similarly subject to doctrine and system. Its premise is that the apprehension of death and exposure to death is the decisive psychological fact of our time. A study of returning Vietnam veterans opposed to the war and troubled in their readjustment to civilian life furnishes the evidence by which the premise is shown to be correct. But is the work history by even the widest definition? Granting that it may be called historical in intention because it deals with selected consequences of a long war, is history needed to justify a hatred of war? In 1914 and again in 1941 learned men argued historically to justify their (temporary) detestation of German music or German philosophy; but the feeling would have been as right or as wrong without the argument. A moral choice ought to be made on its own grounds. As a reviewer avowedly sympathetic to psycho-history was brought to say: "Dr. Lifton doesn't like Vietnam.

*Social problems are accounted by some historians "the ultimate values." See Howard Zinn, *The Politics of History* (Boston, 1970), pp. 20–23.

. . . [But] who is to decide for psychiatry what aspects of history are 'good' and what are 'bad'?"[9]

One might add that the "solution of the problem of war" is not likely to come out of the study of one war. Ireland and the Middle East at war today differ altogether from Vietnam; each has its history, because of which the apprehension of death itself must *feel* different. The feeling may not even be "of this century," owing to religion, nationalism, traditional enmities, and other influences not sufficiently regarded by psycho-historians. What the immediate problems demanding "solution"—poverty, slavery, urban ills—do to harm history is to impose an *a priori* judgment on the facts. You may say that no historian goes to work without a hypothesis "a priori"—a hope or a conclusion. But these he can change in the light of evidence without losing integrity, whereas a moral choice, which is rightly made *a priori,* cannot be changed without disgrace to the maker.

The "culture of the people" is another subject that moves students to alter and adulterate their conception of history. An industrial, egalitarian democracy creates clichés of feeling as well as of thought. When daily experience makes it plain that only large organized groups have public importance, the scholarly observer comes to attribute reality only to persons and events found in quantity. Hence the laborious search through archives for the deeds of the many. The mass age needs mass premises and conclusions.

This sentiment is reinforced by the Marxian ethic. Salvation by class destiny and through inevitable dictatorships by proletariats are dwarfing conceptions that cast out the individual as well as the traditional groupings and interests of Western societies. Political parties, diplomacy, high art and spiritual religion—to say nothing of "civility," the once living elegance of great cities—seem small and contemptible under the wheels of the future. A disguised totalitarianism may thus be at work in the student who thinks that in the past only "the people" deserves notice.* It seems at first unlikely that this emotion congenial to the quantifier should also suit the psycho-historian. But he too puts his trust in a great collective force, the unconscious, which throws into correct perspective the puny conscious wills of individuals and castes. The collective mind reveals and also emancipates the unconscious, defeats all elitism and privacy, and denies the autonomous force formerly discerned in great men: they are driven like the rest and by the rest. In psychic as in materialistic determinism, the actors do not know their real goals, which are decided from below.† Everything "above the line" is but superstructure and illusion.

The Ethics and Politics of Certitude

Yet these tempting avenues of thought do not lead to fatalism. On the contrary, the hope of gaining understanding by going underground, to the depths, is one with the hope of ethical and political transformation. Hence the impatience with mere historians is not the normal dissatisfaction with earlier histories and biographies, but rather with the political and social at-

*Who the people are it is not easy to say from the writings ostensibly devoted to them. Certain minorities appear to represent the whole, on the principle that (1) they have been forgotten and (2) the people has been forgotten, therefore (1) = (2). On this principle, criminals, lunatics, infants, and animals have become the subject of historical studies and esthetic theories, some of them extremely valuable, though not answering to the comprehensive sense of *das Volk*.

†In the late nineteenth-century science of anthropo-sociology mentioned above (p. 6n.), class struggle was seen as the unconscious struggle of races, the participants being unaware of the race to which they belonged, though "science" knew, in accordance with "Ammon's Law" (J. Barzun, *Race, a Study in Superstition*, pp. 159–60).

titudes that went into their composition. Fortunately for the doctrinaire historians, fact and interpretation are sometimes separable, and the incriminated works can provide the raw materials with which the new are fashioned. One powerful incitement to recycling old facts instead of rewriting plain history from a new moral base is the success of "human engineering" that modern society seems to demand and science to aid and abet.*

On the lowest level, the impulse has been a "Me too" demand for computer time. Not the historians alone, but bold spirits in the arts and literature have latterly believed the garrulous machine could transmute their leaden data into golden truths, and they have shoveled their "facts" into the mouth of the minotaur. Their confidence in the result is supported by the now pervasive outlook that might be called domestic anthropology, the belief that our own society is and ought to be an analyzable object. The conviction is so familiar it needs no further description. The language in which the least pedantic people talk about themselves and their difficulties shows how willingly subject is abandoned for object.† The very guardians of the disciplines of wholeness—the so-called humanists—desert in droves

*In a remarkable philosophical work on history, with special reference to Collingwood, Professor Louis O. Mink says: "Historians . . . have more and more been prodded into reflection on their discipline as they have keenly felt the pressure of an imperialistic behavioral science which . . . recommends . . . that they stick to the 'facts' and leave explanations to the methodologically sophisticated social sciences" (*Mind, History, and Dialectic* [Bloomington, Ind., 1969], p. 158).

†The great American popularizer of the anthropological point of view, Dr. Margaret Mead, never made it clearer than when she entitled one of her lectures "Continuing Problems in Biosocial Fit" (College of Physicians and Surgeons, New York, Feb. 4, 1970). A naive, unanthropologized auditor might have hoped that a biosocial fit was what he would like to throw during a dull party; but then he would only become one of the continuing problems.

from their old faith and feverishly apply to their work the techniques of counting, theme analysis, symbol hunting, and reduction to fundamental structures, including myth. Nothing may be left as it is, because the analysts are sure—perhaps by "projection"—that here is the goose with the golden eggs.

This objectifying of life and the lifelike encourages the motives from which it started and excludes their opposites. It is a vicious circle of feeling easy to understand: knowledge derived from "objective" studies increases self-consciousness. New facts and interpretations keep casting doubts on previous findings about self, society, and method as well. Ideas abound, but they are never assimilated, in the sense of being forgotten and *embodied,* so as to afford new strength and freedom. Instead, insecurity worsens and the desire for solutions redoubles. In these conditions little value can be seen in the search for historical truth and all hope is attached to the search for a determinism. It is the sea bottom desperately felt for by the spent swimmer's nerveless foot.

Yet the searchers show confidence, in the characteristic ways of scientific propaganda. They regularly administer the shock of surprise, relate great effects to the small cause—almost unbelievable, it is so remote from common experience—and take frequent satisfaction in the public dismay. This pattern has a respectable history. It emerged with the Enlightenment and was set during the campaign for Darwinism in the 1860s and 70s, when the revelation that the sun was cooling fast brought pleasure to those privileged to announce it first. They were a step ahead of their friends and enemies in the knowledge most important for the needs of the day: brute fact was supposed to settle the fate of all gentler realities—a fallacious transfer to social thought of the principle that in science a fact is enough to destroy a whole edifice of thought.

When Lytton Strachey followed the same form to debunk historic reputations, he believed he was shattering Victorian pieties with a new weapon, but he was only borrowing the motive and the misapplication. Both are still with us, as when, for instance, the *History of Childhood Quarterly* (subtitled *The Journal of Psychohistory*) lures its readers by summarizing an article in these terms: " 'Childhood and the Bible' . . . argues why the Bible is a coherent story of intra-family struggle and asks if the history of the West may not more usefully be described as a part of the history of childhood rather than the other way around."

That such a proposed "description" of Western civilization eliminates the meaning of childhood (by eliminating that of adult) and destroys both the religious and the historical significance of the Bible (by reducing its contents to side effects of the bed and the bassinet) does not seem to occur to these psychohistorians. Their efforts are evidently to *dispose* of history and civilization, of human error and achievement, rather than to contemplate them.* Unwittingly, motive overcomes purpose; the desire to understand is undone by the rival desire to quell uncertainty through reductive ideas.

Fictionism and Preposterism

Ethical and political motives—it must be said again—are legitimate. They can be productive, just as

*"And as for the significance [read into the] fact that after the 1970 predawn chat with antiwar students at the Lincoln Memorial Mr. Nixon ate 'corned beef hash with an egg on it' for the first time in five years ('After the catharsis, an acceptable short regression in orality')—such an insight is enough to give pause to even true believers in psycho-history" (Christopher Lehmann-Haupt, *New York Times,* May 11, 1972).

Mr. Norman O. Brown, the advocate of a return to infantile sexuality, is more consistent than the psycho-historians when he says that psychoanalytic thought is *a way out of history.* See *Life against Death* (Middletown, Conn., 1959), pp. 93 ff.

the young's impatience with the old—"Away with all that!"—is normal and may inspire original work. But a motive springing entirely from local or temporary circumstance will by definition lead only to a parochial or fashionable performance. It seems to be admitted even by psycho-historians that the analytic study of Woodrow Wilson by Freud and W. C. Bullitt was reprehensible journalism.* The difficulty is of course to assess one's motive. But in professing to write history it should not be hard to ascertain whether one retains any deep interest in the material one is working with, or whether one takes it solely as a means to an end—to making a point, including the egotistic point of being a revisionist. The alternative is not simply to remain "neutral," as Dr. Lifton seems to imply in his otherwise excellent statement on the question of motive: "The approach seems to require . . . a considerable ethical concern with the problem being investigated. Erik Erikson has hardly been neutral in his feelings about Luther's achievements or about what Gandhi's legacy may still mean for the world. Nor has Keniston been neutral about student radicals, Coles about minority group aspirations, nor I about Hiroshima and its legacy. Rather, all of us have been struggling toward . . . making conceptual use of these very involvements."[10]

Making conceptual use of ethical feeling requires as much originality and independence of mind as any other part of history-writing, and historians stand or fall by their success in this department. The student familiar with the lives and works of Guizot or Tocqueville will want to compare the conceptual manifestation of their motives with cases nearer our time. They will find that what is rare in the ethically sensitive is the power to rise above current images of moral indignation. For example, a metaphor now in vogue denounces our "sick society" and tempts social critics to

*See Paul Roazen, "Freud and Woodrow Wilson" in *Sigmund Freud,* ed. Paul Roazen (Englewood Cliffs, N.J., 1973), pp. 168 ff.

say that the schizophrenic's response to it is that of a sane man to a mad world. If the historian, in his ethical sympathy with the *purport* of this view, loses his ability to weigh and compare, he may find that nothing stops him from rewriting history as the antics of the pathological or the doings of the nursery. These are his "conceptualizations," even though he may only be writing an article in that vein and not formally subscribing to the explicit idea. Compare the notion common to the psychic and the statistical interpretations, that men are *driven*. Then ask yourself whether you as an individual feel anything like the compulsion that recently led a youth to ask for admission at Bellevue Hospital in New York, saying: "I think I'm going to hurt somebody." He had already killed one person and been confined and treated, then released as cured.[11] The case is far from unique and it suggests that there are degrees in the actuality of being driven.

To equate mankind or the past as a whole with the vividly felt portion of it that involves one's own life is to be neither scientist nor historian. Rather, it is to impersonate the novelist, and this without the safeguards against deceiving the public that literature presented as fiction contains within itself. Indeed, it is the influence of the novel as "truth," it is the respect for art as much as the respect for science, that has weakened native skepticism into accepting the improbable at sight, relishing the offbeat, and preferring denial to confirmation, not because it is justified, but because it upsets. To say this is not to impugn the intelligence of any particular group: the mood is pervasive and any honest thinker will acknowledge this external pressure on his judgment. That is one reason the more for expecting our historians to keep away from all fashions. For them, certainly, it is the only way to frame a message that will carry beyond the half decade in which it is uttered. For the public, it is the only protection against history that flatters prejudice, gloomy or hopeful.* In short, "To make conceptual use of one's involvement" means to look beyond it, to see it from above, and from the next century, and thus to purge one's motive of importunate desires.

The resolve to let one's ethical urge suffuse the work by its own aptness and merit and not by contrivance and system should also get rid of an intellectual error, characteristically modern and self-conscious, which is a form of the *post hoc* fallacy—taking the starting point of an endeavor as a guarantee of what may under certain conditions be its outcome. For example, Hobbes and Machiavelli, moved by a passionate concern about contemporary affairs, achieved profundity and influence. Let us then be passionate about the contemporary in order to achieve greatness and influence.† Similarly, because ideas that were singular and shocking at first have turned out to be true and valuable, therefore a deliberate singularity must mean success. Numerous triumphs of art and science seem to warrant this melodrama of reversal and happy ending. And hence the flood of "findings" whose first and last claim to attention is that they defy judgment and experience. These contortions of research in the study and the historiography of man it would be impossible to parody—they parody one another and satire could only plagiarize reality. But they can be turned to account as lessons in

*"I was sorely tempted when I wrote on Washington in the American Revolution to dwell on the many, many parallels to the Vietnam war. But I resisted such anachronisms partly as a matter of historical conscience and partly out of an egotistical desire to have my book of interest for a longer period of time than the 1960s and 1970s. When I got on the radio or television, I was asked to relate my labors to the news. Again, I refused" ("George Washington and the Watergate Psychology," an address by James T. Flexner at the Century Association, New York, June 7, 1973, p. 7).

†The fact is that *The Prince* and *The Leviathan* were so far from contemporary in *outlook* that they displeased all parties and only gradually attained their present importance.

the theory of motives. It is accepted in esthetics that good sentiments are not enough to produce good literature; it is accepted in morals that will and desire must be fastidious, or the end is compromised. These maxims hold likewise in the realm of intellect. In the effort to make history solve problems—or simply in the effort to write history—it is not enough to have a worthy motive: it must be a motive distilled and purified, just as the method must be genuine and not mere posturing, and the evidence treated with fastidious care. Then, with reasonable luck in other respects, the purpose of the enterprise will at least not be compromised from the outset and may possibly begin to be fulfilled.

5

History as Counter-Method and Anti-Abstraction

Loose Talk about Precise Matters

In common as well as academic speech, the phrases "historical method," the "historian's methods," are current and supposedly well understood. This usage makes plausible the program of mingling or fusing other methods with the historical, though how their elements mesh is not explained. One excellent reason for the omission is that history has no method or methods. This truth is evident if one takes science or industry or accounting or medicine or law or psychiatry for comparison. Each of these has a procedure, a systematic mode of progressing from question to answer, difficulty to remedy, purpose to result. Each has indeed a number of methods, adapted to the variety of purposes and means. There are apparently two ways to manufacture household ammonia, and several to determine atomic weights, file an answer to a charge, audit a business, treat cancer, and recondition a neurotic. All are methods in that they follow a largely predetermined course: they repeat, and it is the repetition, the "normalization" (to use the quanto-historian's term) that insures or gives a high probability of success.

Now the historian only seems to perform in a like manner. The handbooks say: consult your sources, test and authenticate them, assemble the ascertained facts, write your report, and give clear references. After publication another volume is classified as history on some library shelf. But all this is hardly more than a general description of the work of intelligence, such as is performed by every student and professional, with or without a method. Method for the historian is only a metaphor to say that he is rational and resourceful, imaginative and conscientious. Nothing prescribes the actual steps of his work: what defines "his" sources? What tells him where they are and in what sequence he should approach them? What does it mean to "test" them—has he a reagent in a bottle, a casebook, a table of coefficients?* Think of the "scientific" historian Freeman acknowledging that Niebuhr could ascertain the truth by "laborious examination and sober reflection." Think of Woodrow Wilson ascribing Mommsen's greatness to "his divination rather than his learning," which was none the less enormous.[1] To be sure, the historian will be *methodical* in taking notes (though not always) and in reasoning out discrepancies of date or fact; but that is no more than a good bookkeeper does when his accounts do not jibe. On that level it is even possible for the historian to be a poor "bookkeeper" and by other qualities survive his shortcomings.

Let us then abandon the metaphor and leave "method" to those who can show that they possess one in the strict, procedural sense of the term. It will often be found in psycho-history, as our assessment of certain of its claims has shown, that the "method" is only a vocabulary. When mixing terms is as far as the attempt has gone, the inference is strong that history resists any genuine application of method.

*To be sure, an historian may go to a chemist and ask him to analyze a piece of paper to ascertain its composition and thus infer its age and the genuineness of the document. But that is only to make use of another worker's facts, to rely on *his* method, not the historian's—else there would be no need to consult.

The Point of Pascal's "How We Think"

The reason is not, as vulgar suppositions declare, that historians are conservative or prudishly averse to the sexual truths of Id-ology, or short of brains for mathematics. The reason lies in the difference between two orientations of the human mind, the intuitive and the scientific. Pascal, who possessed the genius for both, gave of them a definitive account in his *Pensées*. Whoever wants to understand the difference between, say, Carlyle's *French Revolution* and Crane Brinton's *Jacobins*—why one is a history and the other not*—should turn to Pascal's first chapter and assimilate the series of distinctions set forth there between the *esprit de finesse* and the *esprit de géométrie*. Neither *esprit* is higher or deeper or better than the other. They are only radically divergent modes of conceiving and working with reality.

A compressed paraphrase could run as follows: in science (the geometrical mind), the elements and definitions are clear, abstract, and unchangeable, but stand outside the ordinary ways of thought and speech. Because of this clarity and fixity, it is easy to use these concepts correctly, once their strange artificiality has been firmly grasped; it is then but the application of a method. In the opposite realm of intuitive thought (*finesse*) the elements come out of the common stock and are known by common names, which elude definition. Hence it is hard to reason justly with them because they are so numerous, mixed, and confusing: there is no method.

From the dissimilarity it follows that genius in science consists in adding to the stock of such defined entities and showing their place and meaning within

*Note in passing that the subtitle of Brinton's book is: "An Essay in the New History." Its date is 1930.

the whole system of science and number; whereas genius in the realm of intuition consists in discerning pattern and significance in the uncontrollable confusion of life and embodying the discovery in intelligible form.

Obviously the two modes of thought do not mix well: there are no natural transitions from the one to the other, the *movement* of the mind in each goes counter to the other. This fundamental incompatibility explains why psycho-history and quanto-history are not the improvement of an invertebrate genre by the injection of a stiff dose of method or even a desirable progression away from the parent form. Once understood, the opposition resolves many puzzles and conflicts in contemporary culture, which is torn and racked by the imperialistic demands of each "mind" simultaneously.

How to Tell History from Other Works of the Mind

The distinction once made, it is important not to turn it into a biological postulate. There are not two *species* of minds, only two orientations, comparable to the further differentiations which, within the intuitive group, lead an individual toward music, or the graphic arts, or poetry. The human mind is one: otherwise every sort of thinker or artist would be excluded from the understanding of other sorts. History, again, is not a unique mode of thought, as Collingwood's final philosophy seems to say. Historians think and work like critics and scholars and lawyers and statesmen, when these are not bound by external system. Indeed, the historian shares with the ordinary man of today a common outlook. They are at one on the significance of time, cause, continuity, and development, and that fact in itself is enough to make history what it is.*

*Philosophers of science, such as Professor Henry Margenau of Yale, divide the universe of experience into the *historical* and the *lawful*. This second, ambiguous word means the realm of physics,

What, then, are the criteria by which history may be known? There are four: Narrative, Chronology, Concreteness, and Memorability. History is first of all a story; "interpretation" is optional, and some histories can do without it; for example, Barante's *History of the Dukes of Burgundy*. The "story" is, of course, intended as truth and it gives particulars of change within time and place, the stretch of either being narrow or wide according to choice.

Next, concreteness prevails over any other interest. The event, the what-happened, is the main fare. In that axiom is to be found the difference between history and biography, for biography may be a study of character, ideas, or spiritual states, in which a few private events are pegs for the analysis. This test obviously marks off history from studies of situations, also actual, but not dealt with as events in continuous time; for example, institutional problems, cultural types, or the "anatomy" of comparable conditions, such as revolutions, decadence, slavery, or the status of women. Yet concrete does not necessarily mean physical. There are "events" in the history of culture and they can be described and fitted into a narrative, provided what happened in art or ideas is not abstracted into a series of "problems" and "influences" and divorced from the mundane facts surrounding the cultural.*

Finally, history is the story of what is memorable, in the two meanings of "worth remembering" and "capable of being remembered." This doubly defining clause is very broad; there are no clear limits to what one person or another will deem worth remembering. Yet it is evident that no one wants "all the facts," even if it

---

etc., in which the quantified regularities suggest obedience to a law. The first term, *historical,* means that time is the organizing principle among events and helps define their character: no single, controllable set of conditions can be assigned for what happens (*Open Vistas* [New Haven, 1961], pp. 194–214). On "law" in the equivocal sense, see below, p. 121.

*See Checklist, no. 20.

were possible to collect their traces. The two senses of memorable therefore point, one to selectivity, the other to intelligible pattern.

The definition of history by these four criteria suggests further traits for judging the immense variety of histories. Though the great ones accord with the description, many other works of merit will appear as only in part historical. In books legitimately entitled "A History of . . . ," will be found many kinds of data that "belong" to other disciplines—geography, ordnance, numismatics, medicine, and so on ad infinitum. The stream of truly historical statements gives motion to the rest.* What is more, the historian may pause to comment, explain, argue, speculate, moralize, and compare. Such interruptions of the narrative are often found in the great histories, but the digressions, whether to acclimate the unfamiliar or inject opinion, are not allowed to become ends in themselves. The data of one kind are not gathered from end to end and tabulated for scrutiny and generalization. The upshot of any chapter or part is not a simple formulated truth, but the communication of many truths, in an artful mixture of order and disorder addressed not to the geometric but to the intuitive mind.†

*Burckhardt's *Age of Constantine* and *Civilization of the Renaissance in Italy* are good examples of historical works in which the feeling of movement akin to narrative is not overborne by the topical treatment.

†The two joint reviewers of Professor David Landes's *Unbound Prometheus,* a history of industrial change from 1750 to the present, call the author an "old economic historian, certainly not a new" one. They explain: ". . . although much of what he deals with is susceptible to statistical analysis, to graphing, tabling, and mapping, he firmly remains a historian of figures rather than a statistician of economic change" (*American Historical Review* 76 [1971]: 470). Note the telltale vacillation: he is an old historian; he remains an historian; he declines to be a statistician; he won't graph, he writes. The reader of these pages has the answer: Professor Landes is an historian.

To sum up: History, like a vast river,propels logs, vegetation, rafts, and debris; it is full of live and dead things, some destined for resurrection; it mingles many waters and holds in solution invisible substances stolen from distant soils. Anything may become part of it; that is why it can be an image of the continuity of mankind. And it is also why some of its freight turns up again in the social sciences: they were constructed out of the contents of history in the same way as houses in medieval Rome were made out of stones taken from the Coliseum. But the special sciences based on sorted facts cannot be mistaken for rivers flowing in time and full of persons and events. They are systems fashioned with concepts, numbers, and abstract relations. For history, the reward of eluding method is to escape abstraction.

Interesting, But Is It True?

Absent method and abstraction, how is it possible for history to hold a serious modern mind, educated to value only what is true and precise? That history has its own precision is the right answer, though as in all products of the intuitive mind no one can offer proofs. Truth and precision in history are perceived by those who know. In this particular, history owns affinity with art, poetry, philosophy, and religion, to which few would deny the possibility of precision and truth though they are untestable by rule. Taking them and history together, one can hardly believe that without the enveloping significance they embody and bestow, science and social science would greatly interest mankind.

It may be objected that untestable precision is a contradiction in terms, but that is an error. The precision of science itself ultimately lies in an observer's reading of his instruments; a picture on the wall could be said to hang straight even if yardsticks did not exist: it would be *seen* to hang straight. Instruments only extend the senses and record *degrees* of precision. As to the more or less, Aristotle pointed out long ago that it was a mistake to require of any subject greater precision than it could or need supply—we usually stop at four decimals for π and at two for $. History has no need of mathematical precision because it deals with activity and not process. Activities are what we do and can imagine others having done; processes are what goes on unwilled or unknown. We ask minute detail and close measures in our accounts of process, because without these exact pointers we are not sure *that* we know or *what* we know: the workings of matter are forever closed to our intuition. Whereas the return of the Ten Thousand or the destruction of Carthage needs only to be described to set up within us immediately precise ideas and visions and emotions, the whirling of molecules in a gas occasions no direct insight or sympathy. We understand it only by analogies painfully sought through elaborate devices and expressed in unevocative symbols.

Of history we ask accuracy of another sort. It is of no moment what percentage of the Ten Thousand wore out their boots on the march home. The figure 10,000 has no *numerical* significance. If the army was composed of 9,900 men or 10,200, nothing in Xenophon's history would be changed: only the rough order of magnitude matters. But other details are all-important—the route, the time spent, the dissensions and who and what caused them, the prospects changing from despair to hope, the great cry "The sea! the sea!" when the retreating force climbed the heights of Mount Theches in Armenia. But it is a defect and a loss for history that we no longer know exactly which peak was called Theches.

Because of such uncertainties, history leads some of

its workers into inquiries only appropriate to science. At all times, and especially now because of science, curious minds are charmed by the sport of inference and deduction, which may give knowledge to fill the gaps of evidence and insight.* As the tradition of text criticism shows, a long chain of plausible arguments seems to make up for its fragility by its virtuoso skill. It has the appeal of the detective's demonstration in the final chapter. But solid history can only regard such gymnastics as a curiosity. The historian suspects the chain of might-be's in which every weak link is a threat to truth. He wants not a chain but a network of cross-confirming testimony; for he is not deciphering a code, he is visualizing a scene and a story.

Scope and Texture of History

Just as the edifice of science is not the simple addition of law to law, or that of art the addition of technique to technique, so the achievement of history is not the addition of fact to fact. Bald factual listing punctuated with dates is unfortunately what many history books propose to the young mind, which duly rebels

*The merit of insight for dealing with human affairs is naturally disallowed by social scientists of the quantifying school. But since social complexities visibly include elements that cannot be quantified, some investigators have come to see that to leave out the unquantifiable is to distort the meaning of the rest. Professor Jay W. Forrester of M.I.T. is one such investigator who, while maintaining that modern social predicaments defy intuition, provides a place in his theory for the experienced man of the world with an "intimate working knowledge of the actual systems" (*Urban Dynamics* [Cambridge, Mass., 1969], pp. 113–14). Unfortunately, in his spoken and published attitudes Professor Forrester tends to forget this concession.

More consistent is the position taken by the authors of *Explanation in Archeology*, Watson, Leblanc, and Redman (New York, 1971). For them the "explicitly scientific approach" does not replace or displace historical archeology: "they are complementary not conflicting" (p. 170).

and acquires a solid prejudice against the subject. It is a pity, because the distant, unexperienced past has features in common with the contents of anybody's memory that ought at a certain age to make history assimilable—it presents the same chaotic inclusiveness and disproportion between barely noticed events and the subsequently large result. The principal effect of history is to show the past not as orderly and logical but as a confusion that up to a point can be sorted out and understood.

As the record of events grows in size, by length of time and the research of many workers, the matter has to be divided into kinds—economic, social, diplomatic, military history. The division, for convenience merely, arises from the historian's obligation to investigate and make clear whatever is not ordinary. The history of remote peoples and places requires an account of the terrain, the peculiar customs, government, religion, and weaponry. These exotic subjects forming interludes within the narrative limit the span of time that can be dealt with, or else the number of subjects. In high civilizations, the uncommon proliferates even at home. Endlessly diversified endeavors are the sign and substance of what is called civilization, and history has to subdivide in order to follow these activities in their development. Description becomes increasingly technical: a history of porcelain manufacture will discuss *pâte sur pâte* and a history of philosophy will explain Occam's razor, neither of which occurs in common use or speech. But in the best of such departmental histories some indication is given of the surroundings —political, social, cultural—in which the magnified activity takes place. And by a full return to its original scope, a history of the age or country will reinstate in its account the findings of the single-theme historians.

The desire for that total view abides in Clio's dedicated followers; if the synoptic work is never written, they approximate it in imagination by reading its fragments. That is no doubt why Pliny said: "Historia a quoquo modo scripta est delectat."[2] Any history is better than none. But one may ask in what sense a history is total, or even comprehensive, when it is compelled to select and is further limited by the powers of organization of one fallible mind. The answer is that depicting the interplay of events, accidents, persons, and motives regardless of kind—that is, as they mingled in reality, unclassified—constitutes what is wanted from history. The picture may be well or poorly drawn, that is not so much the point as that the texture of the work shall replace the *linear view* of reality—fact added to fact, event after event, cause next to effect, on a string.

Even when a historian is tempted to *say* it, his own history does not *show* that the Roman Empire declined *because* of Christianity or *because* of the malaria-bearing mosquito. The very explanation of what the Commercial Revolution was (if indeed it ever was one thing) contradicts at sight the assertion that it was *due to* the shift in the herrings' breeding grounds in the North Sea. Similarly, the Industrial Revolution cannot be slimmed down to a point for linkage with Kay's flying shuttle or the "Protestant ethic." Far from wishing to isolate a cause as science and method desire, history strives to assemble the largest possible constellation of conditions;* the greater the number of inner links and outer relevancies, the greater our power to divine past reality.

The reader, it need hardly be said, must not approach this orchestral performance in a geometrical spirit. "History is an imaginative subject," says Professor Christopher Brooke, and in another connection he

*Yet making sure, as William A. Dunning cautioned long ago, that facts wholly hidden from the contemporaries and discovered later by the historian are not included among the effective conditions.

gives an admirable example of it. In a manuscript of the fourteenth century, a view of the role of the Commons in Parliament is set forth "which would have been thought quite daring in the seventeenth century."[3] Accordingly, some scholars have dismissed the work as eccentric and without significance. No one can now know whether it represented any opinion but the author's. But as Professor Brooke rightly insists, it is this very singularity that matters to the historian. First it is a fact, and then it opens vistas upon human society by showing that while the men of an age conceive of nearly everything in a time-bound way, there can be one man who looks outside the walls of the prison, *proprio motu,* culturally undetermined—and undeterred.

The Finesse to Imagine or Re-enact

The famous theory of history propounded by Collingwood (and in part anticipated by Dilthey) asserts that historical understanding takes place when the historian or his reader "re-enacts" the past event.* The expression is of course a metaphor twice over: the re-enacting is purely in the mind and it can furnish only an incomplete impression—fortunately. One would hate to re-live the Massacre of the St. Bartholomew moment by moment. It is vivid and painful enough when we follow the necessarily reduced account on the page. For the recapture of the past in both writing and reading, it therefore seems preferable to use the word *imagine*. And since imaginations differ, so will the past, wholesale and in detail. How then can we know and understand it in a beneficial way?

*For Collingwood and Dilthey, see the former's *Idea of History* in the edition of T. M. Knox (Oxford University Press, 1956); and for a masterly exposition and critique of Collingwood's theory, see Louis O. Mink, *Mind, History, and Dialectic* (Bloomington, Ind., 1969).

Right there is the root of the conflict between historians and the "superseders" of history. The latter fail or refuse to see how the reality of the past differs from the reality of nature, which they can go out and touch. Nature can safely be assumed to be permanent because it has no history; its changes are not historical, but material, and therefore consistent, predictable backwards and forwards on the basis of rules mutually congruent and endlessly verifiable. The past, on the contrary, is an unstable construct of the imagination. The sole force constraining that imagination is "the record," which is haphazard and also a product of the imagination. Hence any man who tries to say without fraud what is or what was will succeed in proportion as he possesses the imagination of the real. The phrase implies that the historian is a reasoning creature, endowed with the pragmatic logic that goes with the *esprit de finesse.* Like the statesman (or for that matter the sagacious citizen), the historian comes to know how in "his period" men are likely to act, things go; and the event, in life or in research, almost always "verifies."

The result of these operations of the mind is that whereas there is one natural science, there are many histories, overlapping and contradictory, argumentative and detached, biased and ambiguous. Each viewer remakes a past in keeping with his powers of search and vision, whose defects readily show up in his work: nobody is deceived. And thus an original history of quite modest merit may contribute to the great body of History. It will remain valuable and true even when it contains errors since corrected. It remains also, by its very aim and bias, as a document indispensable to the history of ideas. Nor does the multiplicity of historical versions make them all false. Rather, it mirrors the character of mankind, which is no more at one in its view of the present or recently endured past than it is about any other subject, including the past past. In short, the diversity of pasts is the best rendering of "the past." Anyone determined to have a single account certified true will obtain it only by collation with the mind of God.

Imagining for the purpose of writing history—or reenacting, if that more energetic term is taken sensibly—necessarily leaves out many events that may or must have happened; they are excluded by the phrase "of the real." The witness's report of seeing a ghost goes into history as the report, not as the ghost. Unremembered dreams, like secret prayers and unsuspected murders, escape the net. To put it in novelist's jargon, the doctrine of history is realism.* This strict view of contents raises yet another difficulty about the mingling of history with depth psychology. An unconscious motive defies deliberate re-enactment, which is the most conscious of activities. And anything such as a hidden motive, which is by definition beyond the reach of the conscious imagination, also breaks the bounds of historical realism. History imparts the unique, the unheard-of, the improbable, the incredible, the revolting, but not the unimaginable.

Historical Reason: Uncommon but Not Special

The philosophic basis of these considerations is that history has its being within the realm of common sense; its judgments, attitudes, and language are those of common sense. It is easy to deride common sense, because the phrase is vague and can be taken to mean the commonplace. But all terms that matter can be pooh-poohed or vulgarized—freedom, love, salvation, and the rest. On serious occasions, indicative remarks

*This borrowing from literature is but a repayment, since the novel as a literary genre has—at least until recently—assumed the guise of a truthful history.

are possible. The language of common sense is that which on principle avoids technical terms and explains those it is forced to admit. Thus the dictionary is an example and an instrument of common sense, and for a normally educated reader a history should not require the use of a dictionary. The difference between a history and any sort of technical analysis is clear: a history he who runs (or sits) may read.

Common sense as an intellectual standard is something else. About it one must first say that much foolishness has been uttered in its name; for example, the argument that what is common sense for a revolutionist is the opposite for a reactionary; or that, for the majority, popular clichés and superstitions are common sense and everything else is fancy talk. But common sense, whose conclusions philosophers refute only by appealing to it (like Descartes), is not to be equated with ignorance and prejudice. Its value may be briefly put if we say *sustained* common sense.

When we look for this power of sharp perception and consecutive thought in certain persons known to us through literature, we probably go to Dr. Johnson or Sydney Smith; we ought to think also of Swift, of Byron in his letters, of Jane Austen, Thomas Love Peacock, Walter Bagehot, Bernard Shaw, W. H. Auden—and all the great historians. The intellectual traits they share are quite uncommon, which is why it has so often been said that common sense is very rare. The common-sense habit of thought starts from a total absence of cant. It is clear vision in common things, and it is marked by a composure akin to the judicial temper; a detachment from ready-made doctrines, which does not prevent the holding of strong convictions; an ability to see through shams, including advanced intellectual ones; a repugnance for sentimentality and other forms of emotional cowardice; and an untaught knowledge of how the world goes, an intuitive "logic of events," these last two formulations being variants of "the imagination of the real."

All these propensities orient the mind away from abstraction. Common sense is not opposed to abstract ideas, but it asks about their function, one at a time, and holds them to it. When Swift ridiculed the tailors of Laputa for making clothes by trigonometry, he was not against mathematics. He was a man of the world who wanted his clothes to fit. One of the tests of the historical sense is a quick awareness of what fits, what is an historical question and what is not. If anybody wonders what Shakespeare thought of democracy or why Shelley and his wife Harriet did not consult a marriage counselor, he had better not choose historiography as a career, though wide reading in history might cure the defect of common sense. Contrariwise, anybody is also miscast who does not see the need for inquiry and interpretation when he encounters in Pepys's *Diary* for January 16, 1661/62: "the Dean and the Colonel, whom I found to be pitiful sorry gentlemen . . ." and: "my lord Cornwallis, a bold profane talking man." No psychology will explain, only social and cultural history will recapture, the actuality of "gentleman" and the meaning of the five period-epithets.

It is curious but not unusual that preoccupation with method often blinds the intelligence to common sense. In trying to gain acceptance for his view of psychopathological determinism in everyday life, Freud was led to say: "I do not seriously believe that any one will make mistakes in talking in an audience with His Majesty, in a serious love declaration, or in defending one's name and honor before a jury; in short, people make no mistakes when *they are all there,* as the saying goes."[4] One feels like asking, Where have you been all your life? Why did you not keep your ears open when people told you again and again of incidents that contradicted your absurd generality?* A comparable example from among the quantifiers is that of the American linguist who, in order to ascertain the most usual ways of speech, drew on the contents of 3,000 letters written to the government by citizens asking for help in family difficulties.[5] He would have been nearer the mark examining entries for a national poetry prize, the diction of modern poetry being what it is. Only common sense could have told him that letters written under such conditions would contain many wordings the reverse of spontaneous or typical. Unfortunately, no reference book can codify the dictates of common sense in alphabetical order.

Clio Is a Public Figure

In avoiding method, system, jargon, the technical, and the invisible generally, history keeps itself accessible for its public purpose. Modern civilization has had to leave science to the scientists, because the busy world remains perforce *innumerate,* but history has never been left to the historians. Open access to their work is of its essence. They are always exposed to the common judgment since they address themselves to it and use its modes of thought imbedded in language. Science cannot help flouting the notions of common sense—it tells us that glass is a liquid and that there is more space than matter in the tabletop. The illumination we derive from pursuing strict definition to such

*Compare the involuted argument by which Mr. Erikson insinuates a raison d'être for his method: "Confession-like remembrances often seem to be the most naively revealing and yet are also the most complex form of autobiography, for they attempt to prove the author's purity by the very advertisement of his impurities and, therefore, confound his honesty both as a sinner and a braggart" (*Daedalus* 97:701). Some autobiographers are dishonest, true, but to doubt the cathartic impulse of confession and its fundamental honesty is not to know the truth about *some* men.

conclusions is too well known to remark upon, and it works to our advantage. But there is need to say what history illuminates and what benefits it confers. The benefits will be gone into rather fully in the next chapter. Here one can state what the illumination is: history takes the product that influential events and persons have deposited or injected into the public mind, and sifts, corrects, and clarifies it.

It takes, for example, labels good and bad that have been haphazardly attached to men or periods in the course of struggle and debate—Renaissance, Baroque, Puritan, Enlightenment, Romantic, Risorgimento, Impressionist—and by reconstructing the scenes, by narrating antecedents and consequences, it creates order and visibility in place of murky confusion. The scrimmage is not turned into a ballet, but the smoke of battle is dispelled and the onlooker's eye directed at what does possess distinct outline and clear succession in time. Thus Impressionism is seen as a group of men (names, dates, fates), a series of events (exhibitions), a critical conflict (derision versus explanatory theory), a collection of works (now in certain museums), and a cluster of techniques and attitudes, all of which had foreshadowings and sequels (now part of the public eye and mind).

This public role of history needs no special promotion. In times of intellectual vigor, history is continually being argued with, contradicted, rewritten. Unlike science, it does not "progress";* it accumulates, in a *progression* related to public interest. Fashion may declare a work or genre of history obsolete; that is usually the manner (or the bad manners) of the new historians

*To be sure, some scientific principles remain unchanged: the wider theory does not destroy the whole of the old but limits its applicability, while at the same time imposing new ways of conceiving and naming the familiar facts. But by and large science puts its pride in rapid obsolescence, even as it works toward a unified system of nature, presumably a fixed, unchanging reality.

of the moment. But the body of good work remains standing, few facts are discarded, though many interpretations. It takes a change of civilization to alter profoundly the conception of history as such. And even such a cultural chasm is in retrospect easily bridged: Lucian's idea of history is as tenable today as Gibbon's or Michelet's, Christopher Brooke's or G. R. Elton's.

What revision accomplishes over the short span is to throw into relief kinds of facts formerly neglected or undervalued. The resulting shifts in weight and visibility among elements will uncover new aspects of well-known trains of circumstance; the key signature is changed and new harmonies emerge, but the marks on paper do not sound an altogether new tune. For instance, the "revolt" against the idea that there was such a thing as the Renaissance, the "refuting" of Burckhardt's great book, was valuable in that it redirected research and brought out evidence about forerunners and survivals. The late Middle Ages experienced a renewed vogue. There is always an "underside" to every prevalence. But a careful reading of Burckhardt (notably the first chapter of Part III) shows that he was not blind to what was later urged against him, merely less interested in it than in other things.

Revision of another sort occurs when the march of events themselves suddenly throws a portion of the past into a new shape. For example, the treaty England made to end the Boer War was praised for half a century as the ideal liberal, nonpunitive peace—until it was seen that by leaving the defeated Dutch bigots in power, it entrenched their illiberal policies, notably *apartheid*. Or again, the whirligig of time has shown up many of the proud mechanical triumphs of the nineteenth century (including the flush toilet) as the enemies of man in this generation, by polluting air, sea, and land. In this sense history is reversible as science is not. If we add to this peculiar phenomenon the unpredictable discovery or new use of documents, there is enough reason for the perpetual rewriting of history. Its permanence and mutability combined is not the least of its unique features, as it is also the source of its resistance to method and abstraction. The "verdict of history" is sometimes changed with finality because of irrefutable evidence. But more often it is the orientation that is new—the mountain suddenly seen SSE. The fresh view is no more final and exclusive than former ones are sufficient or obsolete.

Seeing this openness and inconclusiveness, psycho- and quanto-historians are naturally tempted to enter the free-for-all, hoping to regulate it. Why not throw into the fray one more report, drawn from a new "level" and capable of settling certain points. The authors of *History as Social Science* admit that there is "some risk" to the "scholarly soul" of the historian "who leaps from psychoanalysis in revolutionary Algeria to the interpretation of the Chinese response to European pressure a hundred years earlier, or from Nazi concentration camps to American plantation slavery."[6] It is also admitted, as we saw earlier, that the "new levels" are sure to be inconclusive too.* That "defect" would not upset the historian. What bothers him is the misunderstanding of history's proper role.

That misunderstanding is twofold: (1) the new "levels" are not really open to public inspection: the language of the new interpretation is arcane, not even common to all the experts; and (2) the new levels of understanding do not really converge—to use another theorist's word—with those of history proper. Public judgment is thus diverted from the substance of history to the spectacle of experts disputing "with all the uncertainties," as one historian politely puts it, "that are the inevitable concomitant of trained intelligence."[7] (The

*See p. 63.

word *trained* is the polite touch.) It is the kind of intelligence—and here the public is not diverted but bewildered—which can "leap" from Algeria to China and Nazis to slaveholders and reach a tenable conclusion. Conceivably, it could also answer the question about Shakespeare's view of democracy. It is not the historical intelligence.*

The Democracy of Interest

In the definition of that intelligence—which is the subject of this entire book—is implied the maxim "Every man his own historian." What it declares is a plain fact: no one can make the citizen meet a minimum standard of historical knowledge as one can make him know enough to be an electrician or a druggist. Everybody owns the random amount of history he has earned or inherited. Yet it is in the public interest—as will be suggested in the next chapter—that everyman should carry in his head something more than the unexamined history of his own life. To this end, "public interest" has to be taken in its other meaning of interesting to the public. History should be good reading, without vulgarization or talking down. The alteration of history by specialisms therefore poses the question whether the intellectual life is to lose its last general medium of discourse, not common speech on the one hand, and not technical discourse on the other. For in the social sciences the specialist has won hegemony and reaches the public not at all, or else watered down by journalism.

It was not always so. Most of the great works

*To prevent the supposition that historians dislike psychological speculation, one must assert that they often indulge in it, being careful to label it speculation and not fact. When facts support the speculation, the historian will not claim to have pierced a secret. History is not made up of secrets, though the mind of man remains unfathomable.

of sociology and anthropology that have shaped Western man's idea of himself—Machiavelli's *Prince,* Montesquieu's *Spirit of Law,* Adam Smith's *Wealth of Nations,* Burke's *Reflections on the French Revolution,* Malthus's *Essay on Population,* Carlyle's *Past and Present,* Henry Mayhew's *London Labour and the London Poor,* Frazer's *Golden Bough*—addressed the educated. They achieved a greater coherence of thought than our scattered and overblown reports and fed the mind on ideas that could be both understood and criticized.* These advantages were due in large part to the social sciences' tradition of historical discursiveness. When Marx was directly effective, it was because he wrote historical pamphlets or because someone had extracted the historical passages from *Das Kapital.* In the same way, Macaulay in his famous third chapter gave an intelligible "sociology" of England in 1685, not a set of statistics about it. Figures would have been hard to find, but that was not his reason for preferring words. Had he "graphed and tabled" the data for his chapter, it would have been either skipped or studied, not read.†

The Democracy of Contents

If common readability is required for such a public act as history, its interest for the public requires in turn the depiction of things both like and unlike the famil-

*See pp. 129–30 for the intelligent yet inevitable misunderstanding of a famous modern report of national and international importance.

†More artful even than other historians, Macaulay put his survey of living conditions not at the beginning of his book but after two chapters of rapid storytelling. The first begins with the Romans in Britain and brings us to the seventeenth century. The second builds up momentum at the pace set for the remainder of the work, takes us to the death of Charles II, and by the suspense inherent in the issues set forth carries us safely over the necessarily static third chapter.

iar. We noticed above the motive that impels modern students to investigate the destinies of "the people," their deeds and thoughts and how they earned their living. The arduous effort is often accompanied by a sermon on the immorality of writing other kinds of history, especially the political. This call to virtue has once or twice been in order, but since Voltaire's essay *On the Customs and Manners of Nations* (1756) and even more since Herder, Michelet, and the Romantic-Liberal school, historians in the West have grounded their histories on the firm base of ordinary life. Their subjects are peoples and societies. Political history remains the indispensable framework, but with an enlarged significance that overlaps and leads into economic, social, and cultural history. King-and-battle narration has long since disappeared; it is kept alive only as a memory and only by those who damn it.

The great histories have been neither exclusive nor one-sided. They have shown the conditions of life for high and low, rich and poor, and they have fashioned their narrative around the deeds of those who stood out from the mass. For history is about the active minorities to which the majorities yield or consent. This is not an arbitrary choice. There is a natural limit to what can be said about the way people earn their bread, get married, entertain themselves, worship their gods, and pursue *uneventfully* their path to the grave.* In great events the people becomes protagonist. The historian follows the evidence. Froude's *History of England,* which spans the sixteenth century, is an excellent example. It begins with a hundred pages on feudalism, population, the poor laws, trade, the decline

*This limitation is not overcome even in histories of popular or primitive culture. The narrator selects what best exhibits the activities of the group he is describing—the best pot or ballad, the most talented improviser or medicine man. These are necessarily different from the average and the failures, yet representative.

of towns, labor and capital, religion and irreligion, prices, the education of the poor, archery and other amusements, the handloom weavers, and another three dozen topics related to the common life. There is even a long footnote reproducing an inventory of furniture and other belongings.

Then Froude moves on to affairs of church and state and diplomacy, reverting to the people in England, Ireland, and Scotland whenever they act or respond to events and ideas outside their daily round. The Pilgrimage of Grace, for instance, dealt with at great length, brings up the condition of the country poor, women, farm prices, *and* the effect of a religious revolution, led from above, on all the classes of society. It is hard to imagine what other manner of proceeding could be adopted.

Men as Real Agents

Whether attention should be given to "great men" is a question superficially related to the previous one.* There is a lobby against their continued appearance in history. The manifest motive is to avoid anything that savors of elitism, for an elite is less than the whole. But a no less potent motive is the fatalist assumption about the course of human events: great men are illusions, mere façades for the real forces or "factors."† This is one of those circular reasonings that need only to be grasped to be seen as fallacious: it is a geometrical kind

*The phrase needs quotation marks to make clear that all it means is prominent, leading, dominating men, not necessarily geniuses.

†The ancients, who thought they knew the effect of leaders, good or bad, on the fortunes of the city, thought of history as rewarding heroism with fame and inspiring the young to emulation. Compare a psycho-historian's interpretation of the hero: "All wars seem to require heroes around which civilian populations can cleanse themselves of guilt and reassert immortalizing principles" (Robert Jay Lifton, "Heroes and Victims," *New York Times*, Mar. 28, 1973).

of error. The starting point is: if Napoleon had not existed, somebody else would have done what he did, the "real forces" being there. One reason for so saying is that the job done was so tremendous, no one man could have done it—it was bound to be done. But to say this is to imply that one is sure of the course of events: they are inevitable, and one is in effect foretelling what happened. But it is clear that such a forecast was not possible, since Napoleon, who had *some* relation to the events, could not have been predicted. On the one side, then, the argument boils down to saying that Napoleon was not involved at all. In his absence a similar character would have taken his place; and on the other side, the support for this last statement is that the results were bound to happen—inevitable and predictable. But that was the very point to be proved, which the argument has *dis*proved.

There are other, empirical ways of showing the part played by individuals in history, for example, the sudden change in the cohesiveness of a group or the firmness of a policy when he who leads and directs is removed. It is not illusion or prejudice that causes historians to write, in many contexts, such statements as: "The death of Saladin in 1193 plunged the Orient in civil war and altered the balance of power between East and West." Or again: "By severe but just repression, Henry IV in one year put an end to dueling in France, but his policy lapsed with his assassination and it was not until Richelieu, etc., etc." To be psychological for a moment, it is obvious that one man supplies at least unity of plan, which is a force in itself.* The assertion

*"It might long ago have been predicted with great confidence that both Italy and Germany would reach a stable unity if some one could but succeed in starting the process. It could not have been predicted, however, that the *modus operandi* in each case would be subordination to a paramount state rather than federation, because no historian could have calculated the freaks of birth and fortune

that great men are real forces does not of course imply omnipotence. Circumstances predispose; other men —and the passage of time—help or hinder. History is the means by which we may learn of these contingencies in exact detail, because it resists the fictional appeal of secret causes or dark conspiracies, and because it is not a mindless mechanism. If it were, the "real forces" themselves could not logically be men at all but must be matter.

What Is "The" Historian?

The distinctive features of history have been set off by contrast with other disciplines and orientations of mind. Now we ask what virtues and talents are called for in the historian. The love of fact is indispensable but insufficient. Truth does not reside in a collection of facts; truth is shown by the form of their presentation, once their significance has been seized on. In the record, little of all this is *given.* Telling the truth, then, requires sagacity and style, art in composition and skill in exposition.

From the days of Lucian, at least, it has been said that the chief moral qualities of the historian are worldliness and independence of mind. The peculiar judgment needed to assess evidence comes from knowing men and affairs, which in turn comes from experience: the best historians tend to be men acquainted with public life and over forty years old. The management of affairs helps develop the art of discerning patterns, for administration depends on executing and detecting plans. And it is by its plan that in history the master-

---

which gave at the same moment such positions of authority to three such peculiar individuals as Napoleon III, Bismarck, and Cavour" (William James, "Great Men and Their Environment," in *Selected Papers on Philosophy,* Everyman ed., pp. 188–89).

piece is achieved. As Macaulay broods over his work in his diary, he keeps reminding himself that the arrangement is all-important; it alone makes the welter intelligible and retainable.[8] Composition is, on the large scale, what we are all so tender about on the small scale when we complain of our words being taken out of context. Without the right placing of each part, chronology is muddled, concreteness blurred, narrative stymied, and memory baffled. Great diggers and collectors of fact have sometimes published as history unorganized compilations of findings; they are even less readable than the driest chronicle, for they rebuff understanding whereas the chronicle only fatigues attention. Such works are only useful as quarries for later writers and can set no precedent about form.

Form is not a merit at everyone's command. There is no method for acquiring it. Order and linking are found by absorption and rumination. Our good friends, the theorists of *History as Social Science*, exclaim with dismay: "It is almost as though some scholars felt that historians are born not made."[9] The remark shows the extent to which the creative element in the writing of history has been overlaid and forgotten. It is now assumed that Thucydides, Tacitus, Gibbon, Tocqueville, Macaulay, Henry Adams were "made" and can be reproduced in large numbers with the normalization of methods—or else that they are not true historians, only great ones. Could it be that there lurks here an unwitting desire to parallel the expansion of science by making room for a mass of competent technicians, abandoning—indeed decrying—the role of the born historian?

It will not do to think of such things. Yet there is precedent for having to do so. When in 1904 Woodrow Wilson delivered his great judgment on Mommsen he may have been answering some argument to the same effect; he was certainly taking cognizance of the increasing output of the graduate schools: "How would you critically distinguish it [the *History of Rome*] from a doctor's thesis? By its scope, of course; but its scope would be ridiculous if it were not for its insight, its power to reconceive forgotten states of society, to put antique conceptions into life and motion again, . . . and see a long national history singly and as a whole. Its masterly qualities it gets from the perceiving eye, the conceiving mind of its great author, his divination rather than his learning. The narrative impresses you as if written by one who has seen records no one ever deciphered. . . . Its insight is without rule and is exercised in singleness and independence. It is in its nature a thing individual and incommunicable."[10]

The Inevitability of Literature

The rarity of great historians is due to the infrequent coming together of the many talents they must possess. The worldly man may lack imagination, or the judicial temper, or the power of solitary industry among books and papers. If he has all three he may still be an indifferent writer. He will then fail. It has been fashionable for a good while to affect scorn for "literary history," sometimes concealing more sensible criticisms under the epithet. To one critic, it means fantasy overpowering a feeble sense of fact.[11] To others it means good prose, suspect *a priori* because irrelevant to science.* We should really stop using the adjective as if it pointed to a definite kind of work. "Literary" means using letters and words. Where is the history that is not a piece of writing, including the studies that stitch to-

*In his witty yet closely argued essay, "The History Schools," Frederic Harrison parodies this species of critic: " 'Literary history!' . . . why not say melodious science! —delicious philosophy! —graceful law! —or any other paradoxical confusion of metaphors? 'Literary history' is a contradiction in terms, is it not . . . ?"(*The Meaning of History* [New York, 1902], p. 131).

gether layers of history with graphs and diagnoses? The *literary* fact is that poor writing, wherever found, conceals or distorts or destroys the truth. The historian, who has no business being a numerator, must be a denominator.*

For him, research is an encouragement to clear exposition. Unlike the methodists and abstractionists, he is at all times close to his materials. Their "feel," their enormous diversity, is an education in itself. It compels the mind to find expression for the differences perceived and to struggle for the grouping and shading that will reproduce the impression they make. This exercise of the visual and the verbal imagination is akin to the self-discipline of the realistic novelist, with the added constraint of factuality.

This analogy is supported by the work of Flaubert. Whereas the abstract opinions on politics and society he expressed in his letters are inconsistent and exaggerated, the scenes from the revolution of 1848 that he wove into *L'Education sentimentale* are admirably proportioned, vivid, without excess, and telling without commentary. They are partly an eyewitness account, partly the result of careful research. Flaubert had the historian's passion for fact and devoted much time to historical research before writing each of his novels.

A long apprenticeship in reading and writing coupled with a public career would seem to preclude the new kind of research—the exhaustive recovery of evidence from "neutral" records. If two lifespans are required, the writing of history must become impossible. And the difficulty is not only one of time: what happens to a fine intelligence when subjected for years to a diet of archives? Quantification may be for such a mind the only recourse after ankylosis of the imagination has

*In his "Treatise on the Way to Write History" (ca. A.D. 160) Lucian includes the art of composition and the ability to write prose free from jargon.

set in. The condition is comparable to that of the old-fashioned antiquarian who knows more on his subject than any man living and dies undelivered of his burden. This is not to say that patient research is not needed for writing history, but that the encyclopedic ideal—all the facts—is self-defeating when it takes the form of multiplying minute proofs of one proposition.*

Even in sociology the field is sampled, not covered. In historiography, anyone who has scanned newspapers extensively to show a state of opinion knows that after a time the evidence repeats itself. There is no need to rout incredulity beyond its normal limits. In a like manner, the judicial temper ends in paralysis unless it is matched by the desire to propose a new truth vividly seen and strongly expressed. Piling up cases from the county courthouse provides a retreat for the mute antiquarian and overjudicial minds combined. Such temperaments are refugees from life, the life the historian must lead, even at the risk of error and incompleteness, if he is to delineate the past. For whatever else life was, it was not cloistered—or confined to the documented facts it strewed along the way.

The Quest for the Immutable

Vague as may be the criterion of "life," the deviations from it are easy to recognize. In the modesty of the molelike pursuit of truth lurks the egotism of believing that mole-method has at last caught its prey and justified the mole-role. But where is the work? The making and unmaking of small points should never be despised, but "research" may be questioned like any other activity long taken for granted. What is to be the end of revision and refutation and substitution, if the building of the edifice out of the small parts is always left to other ages? Actually, the desire to make the

*On the encyclopedic ideal, see Gaetano Salvemini, *Historian and Scientist,* and Checklist, no. 4.

single brick indestructible conceals a vast indifference to its utility, an indifference that the whole organization of academic and scholarly life tacitly supports. The printing press relieves everybody of the need to contemplate what has been found. History, which was once the sum of collective and individual memories, is now delegated: we let the bookshelves remember for us. What has taken so much pains to dig out and package will surely last forever—nobody will care to touch it. If this means that the lifelong diggers have no time left to understand and enjoy their own discoveries, well, they are no worse off than the great public around them, who also live by data without contemplation. To the observer, the upshot of this vast, hopeful, arduous effort is heartbreaking: the existence of the new truths is as abstract as the principle on which they were got; and far from the promised eternity, they live their short day only in the minds of fellow students eager to supersede them with their own ephemeras.

It is the consciousness of this futility that drives strong historical minds to seek the laws of history. If such an enterprise could succeed, all the labors of all previous workers would be redeemed, the great investment of patience and genius would bring a high yield in the form that everybody, laymen and methodists included, yearns for—understanding, explanation, the ultimate Why answered side by side with an account of the stupendous How. No one would then question the utility of history, nor could withhold his attention from it. The ravishing Clio would need no doctors, but rather—like Penelope besieged by suitors—a bodyguard. The product of this desire bears the name "philosophy of history."*

*This accepted term is not to be confused with philosophic discussions of the nature of historical knowledge, such as one finds in Burckhardt, Dilthey, Collingwood, Arthur Danto, and others, including some of the "philosophers of history" in the other sense of the term.

The several versions are familiar. In modern times Bossuet, Vico, Herder, Comte, Hegel, Buckle, Marx, Gobineau, Spengler, Toynbee, W. H. McNeill have taken on the task and left works still to be reckoned with. The expenditure of learning has been prodigious—and it is not ended. The appeal of system is indestructible, but not—alas—the system. For it is not a paradox to say that in seeking a law of history those passionate minds were giving up their interest in history. They were drawn on to something else, possibly something "higher," but deserting history was their undoing. The sad contortions and false simplicities of all the philosophies of history so far written are enough to disqualify them at the base—no need to go further and ask for the promised "laws." The largest, most learned and sustained effort is undoubtedly Toynbee's *Study of History* in ten volumes (1934–54). Yet one needs no profound knowledge of the history of any one place or period to find in it not indeed "historical errors"—they are found in all historians—but fatal cracks in the structure.* Abstract systems spell failure in history *ipso facto;* history and ideology wage the Hundred Thousand Years' War. As Professor J. H. Plumb put it with finality, to the historian "ideological interpretations, Marxist or nationalist, conservative or liberal, religious or agnostic, providential or progressive, cyclical or linear, are a violation of his discipline and an offense to his knowledge."[12]

In spite of its irremediable defects the philosophy of history, like other aberrations of misplaced love, has not been without benefits. It proceeds from the spirit of

*For a critique of its metaphysical presuppositions, see H. R. Trevor-Roper's review, reprinted in *Men and Events* (New York, 1957). Historical objections can be sampled in Pieter Geyl's *Debates with Historians* (The Hague, 1954).

absolutism, but it is not one of those imports rendered incompatible by their technique or idiom. In some attempts, the "law" is but a rash overextension of "pattern." In the justly famous philosophies the reader can relish the narrative passages and will gratefully cull the sudden insight, the new concept and its descriptive term. The language not only of history but of general culture has adopted the most useful of such creations: *Zeitgeist,* "world-historical character," "Faustian culture," "ages of criticism and ages of creation," and others that will readily occur. It is now hard to imagine how we could have done without them. But students of history have not taken them at their face value; the terms have been naturalized into the common tongue, like other metaphors of past and present psychologies.

Among these borrowings the central one, "law," is not enlightening but productive of superstition; for it echoes the misleading language of science and strengthens the confusion between a man-made social ordinance and a generalized statement of observed fact.* There is no *law* of gravitation that stones and plunging suicides "obey." The word is a poor analogy and thrice ambiguous. In science any verified exception to a "law" would at once destroy it; whereas in society a thousand violations leave the law just what it was. The difference between science and history, it was said before, is that the one deals with processes, the other with activities. Science can say: x therefore y; history never dares to say the same, or its equivalent: only y comes out of x. The connections are undetermined. Hence the philosopher who, scientist-like, gazes at history and sees a grand design in its unfolding, shows that he takes men for stones acted upon and

*Recall the regrettable and now widespread usage by which philosophers of science call nature the realm of the lawful and everything else the realm of the historical (see note, p. 93n.).

not acting. And in using the concept of law he also takes stones for voluntary agents that "obey" an external rule. In short, entangled in metaphors and false assumptions, he denies reality to history's most conspicuous feature, which is *active change.*

6

The Formative Effect of History

No Lesson, Then, for Next Time?

There is no point in writing history if one is always striving to overcome its principal effect. That effect —need it be said again?—is to show the contents and character of the past, its vagarious, "unstructured" disorder, due to the energetic desires of men and movements struggling for expression and full sway. Hence the futility of trying to make history say something positive in answer to system and method. Histories are imperfect mosaics, unofficial reports, held together by a "logic of events" which is clear to writer and reader because of their own animal faith in motive and reason. History is possible because earlier men have left traditions, affidavits, monuments consonant with that same faith. By the imagination of the real, historians discern regularities and individualities and give to each in their work the shapes appropriate to time and place, including the time and place of writing. But, in the end, multiplicity defeats regularity and no one can turn from the record or the history feeling that "now he knows." Truth is a relative term, here as always, an abbreviation of "truthfulness."

Of what use, then, these flawed pictures and scripts? What can man or society gain from attending to them, when so much is to be done here and now and other keen minds are at work producing the knowledge with which to do it?

The use of history is for the person. History is formative. Its spectacle of continuity in chaos, of attainment in the heart of disorder, of purpose in the world is what nothing else provides: science denies it, art only invents it. To try to make out the same vision for oneself in the midst of life is difficult, not to say discouraging. One might suppose that an astute synthesis of the items in the daily paper would supply it, but the paper lacks charm and solidity; its formative effect is nil, as one can see from sampling public opinion. Reading history remakes the mind by feeding primitive pleasure in story, exercising thought and feeling, satisfying curiosity, and promoting the serenity of contemplation. Nobody can read, even in part, the histories of Caesar, Clarendon, Guizot, Ranke, Motley, Mommsen, Maitland, or Roztovtzeff and be the same person afterwards. There is no way to trace or name the change, which may be slow and gradual; but it is as palpable as that which follows a great artistic experience; it is a spiritual transformation without a creed. The reader is still free. He has been made more extensively conscious, but this new consciousness is absorbed into the old, it is not a fresh burden and not exclusive; a reader of history does not read *a* history, or one for each period: *he reads history.*

If to the beholder the deeds soon become more interesting than the explanations, this influence of the primary realities does not mark a decline in intellect or seriousness. It means rather that the reader is confident about the historical effect. Like the accomplished lover of an art, he immerses himself in the material without scruple. In other words, history is a means of cultivation much more than of instruction. The degree of the difference may be illustrated by a passage from Walter Scott, to whom Clio owes as much as he to her: "A lawyer without history or literature is a mere mechanic, a mere working mason; if he possesses some knowledge of these, he may venture to call himself an architect."[1] For "history" in the first sentence substitute "rural sociology" and the idea turns absurd. To be sure, anybody is at liberty to find principles—to read a lesson—in the history he knows well, but it never stays put. The great commonplaces are all valid: "History repeats itself." But "change is the law of life." "The lesson of history is that men never learn from history." They never learn, but "those who cannot remember the past are condemned to repeat it."[2] These maxims contradict one another because they erect particular afterthoughts into universal propositions.

Permanence out of Instability

Yet this irreducible pluralism forbidding unitary lessons does not keep history from speaking out clearly and comprehensively. As Joan Evans said: "All knowledge is based on tradition; we inherit not only a mass of received opinion which it is easy to accept, but also a mass of refuted hypotheses which it is easy to set aside. Neither empiricism nor experiment can be independent of this tradition, even when their relation to it is contradictory."[3] A single word may embody a tradition and revive it in us; remember in the modern description of Lord Mohun's character the use of "*baleful* star"; or again consider the dictionary identification of "William Joy, the English *Samson,* strong man and smuggler." The Bible was for centuries *the* history with the aid of which ideas simple and complex, practical and awesome were kept in communication.

Because of this power to hand down meanings, history has been condemned for promoting political conservatism. To begin with, this assumes that no former state of things is worth conserving (which should not please the conservationists), and secondly, the charge is inexact. History may be used and misused in support of all conceivable views. The believer in inevitability, discussed in the last chapter, can be a fatalist conservative or a fatalist revolutionary. Believers in human freedom are equally prone to use history. Magna Carta, the Glorious Revolution of 1688, the *principes de '89*, the thought of the Founding Fathers—all have been present appeals to the past for the sake of voluntary change; from which the paradox emerges that revolutionists can be as reactionary as they are futurist. Finally, no one needs history in order to be a political conservative: the eternal truths of religion or of natural law or some other nonhistorical sanction are sufficient warrant.

The tendentious uses of history are less interesting than the resilience that allows them to be made. In spite of its impermanence on many points and lack of finality on all, history has a peculiar robustness. Even when whole ages neglect other ages—the neoclassical ignoring the medieval—or when a great work (such as Tacitus' histories) goes into eclipse, the age, the work, returns, to give justification or warning.*

This continuity of history comes from man's permanent need for a political order. But the forms of that order across time and space differ so much that they disconcert belief. Looking back, the observer is hypnotized at the sight of the Ottoman or Aztec polity, amazed at the magic of its life. The extant descriptions give clues which are interpreted in histories and make these undiscardable. Compared with descriptions, "principles" are empty. Psychology through the ages has offered handy analyses, but we do not read old psychologies—except Burton's *Anatomy of Melancholy*. All others are a closed book. Let a man read history and he is not more sure, but he is wiser. As Trevelyan says,

*Tacitus, for example, began to speak again with deadly cogency when the Western world after the Second World War took in the magnitude of the dictatorships' degradation of civilized life. See Lionel Trilling's "Tacitus Now" in *The Liberal Imagination* (New York, 1950), pp. 198–204.

"When a man has studied the history of the Democracy and the Aristocracy of Corcyra [in Thucydides] . . . his political views may remain the same, but his political temper and his way of thinking about politics may have improved, if he is capable of receiving an impression."*[4]

An Antidote against Cultural Poisoning

Assuming receptivity, history exerts its many-sided formative and reformative effect. It heightens resistance to the superstitions of the day, the flood of conventional knowledge—all of it plausibly wrong—that the surrounding sources of information keep spreading like a sterile sort of manure over contemporary thought. To believe that the persecution of witches was rife in the early Middle Ages "before the rise of scientific ideas"; that France was not prosperous but impoverished in 1789; that ancient Greece was a peace-loving democracy, peopled entirely by artists and patrons of art; that murder has for centuries been punished by death, and property similarly protected because valued as highly as life; that Magna Carta is the original charter of democratic rights, that scientific discovery precedes technological advance; that the first universities were established to teach the liberal arts and did teach them; that Roman law is the antithesis of the English Common Law and contributed nothing to it; that Machiavelli was a ruthless, immoral cynic, Macaulay an apologist for the Whig interest, and Plato a liberal rationalist; that until Darwin nobody knew about evolution and that only after him did religious faith begin to totter; that Hegel was the theorist of Prussian state tyranny and Nietzsche an advocate of world conquest by Nordics; that as the year 1000 ap-

*Burckhardt is even more emphatic: "Not more clever for the next time, but wiser forever."

proached all Europe feared the end of the world—to believe these and a hundred other pieces of "common knowledge" causes error and blindness in current decisions about science, religion, art, education, criminology, revolution, and social action generally.* There need be no conscious reference to the beliefs; they act as the accepted base, or rather as the springboard, from which "educated" thought takes flight.

In the struggle against conventional ideas the historian or biographer is often leader of the opposition. His strength is that he wields the weapon of fact. Thus it was Froude who in 1882 made the great break with Victorian ideas of biography by publishing the facts of Carlyle's domestic life—not, like Strachey thirty-five years later, in a spirit of snickering malice, but out of a finer notion of life and genius. The force of his innovation is measured by the storm of obloquy that fell on the "false friend and biographer." Nietzsche recognized this power of history ("it always enunciates new truths")[5] and rightly attributed it to the restlessness of the historical mind, its urge to throw back all the known facts into the cauldron and recast them into a new significant form.

History enables the independent mind to criticize also the advanced attitudes that misread the present from ignorance of the past. All the novelty-hunting that is later seen as faddishness, and not discovery, is assessed sooner and more truly by the mind ballasted with history. For one of the follies of the emancipated is the belief that the birth of human reason is coeval with their own and that only by their efforts will mankind be rid of superstition. Imagining monsters of error in the

*To take at random a pair of these misconceptions: loss of faith in God is the theme of an early thirteenth-century poem, widely read in its day, by Wolfram von Eschenbach. Wagner sentimentalized it into religiosity 550 years later. The quite imaginary "Fear of the Year 1000" figured as a proof in a psychiatric study of the dying patient in 1955.

past, they overvalue their own fresh proposals and attitudes, and in their name persuade men to acts and opinions as inept or unjust as those they supplant. Too often the new is old error painted over, and the indignation that sustains it blinds the projector to drawbacks and difficulties. But indignation is a poor statesman, and history is the proper cure for that particular inflammation of the ego.

An Antidote against Credulity

In the conduct of life, moreover, the most difficult choice is not simply what to believe but what mode of thought to trust that leads to belief. The temptation is again to let public opinion make that choice. Today, the validity of research expressed in numbers parallels the validity of the democratic count in voting. Politically and intellectually figures must be right. Statistical averages are put forth by the statisticians themselves as descriptions of reality, as historical fact. The public, heedless of the distinction between a vote and an average, an actual count and a sampling, a situation and a tendency, visualizes a state of things instead of a probability and thus bases on thin air reasons for belief and action.

This self-deception is particularly rife in so-called educational research, where the sense of evidence is at its feeblest and the knowledge of history apparently nonexistent. The famous report on Equality of Educational Opportunity (Coleman Report) of 1966 is a case in point. It stated that "our schools have great uniformity insofar as their effect on the learning of pupils is concerned. . . . [S]chools bring little influence to bear on a child's achievement that is independent of his background and general social context." The responses to this revelation by persons of great intelligence and judgment, including Mr. Joseph Alsop, spokesmen for

President Johnson and Senator Robert Kennedy, and a writer for *Science,* were: (1) if the report is correct, the money spent on improving schools is going down the drain; (2) now we know that schools are not the cure; and (3) in view of the American tradition about public schools, the findings are of revolutionary significance.[6] From then on, the nation and the world *knew for a fact* that schools were useless.

Had each man been truly his own historian every intelligent citizen would have known what schooling in the past has done to counteract "background" and "general social context." The story of innumerable illiterate immigrants' offspring who now occupy leading positions in business, the professions, and public life would not have been inwardly suppressed because "test figures show . . ." These persons' very names —Italian, Polish, Swedish, Armenian, and other— would have spoken for the effect of schools. In short, this country's history since Horace Mann would not have been thrown to the wolves of statistics without a second thought.

The tale so far is bad enough, but it has two further twists. After the first shock, the report began to be questioned on grounds of statistical technique. Thereupon—not in public but among experts—it began to be defended for what it was: an analysis of standardized achievement tests given to 600,000 children, which showed a great variation of scores across the country and a similar variation within each of the tested schools. Ergo (perhaps), schools are not far apart in their effectiveness. But ergo (certainly), the "revolutionary" conclusion "schools make no difference" was nothing but sophisticated error.

The second twist came six years later, when a worldwide survey by the International Association for the Evaluation of Education produced a report negating the great alarm of 1966. Interviewed, Dr. Coleman agreed that the new results "suggest to me somewhat more hopefulness about schooling than we had in the past."[7] This unabashed "we" is a lesson in social philosophy for those devoid of history. For to make schools compensate for "background" as they have done in the past is an option forever open, before and after all reports.

What permits the wide acceptance of study after study, with or without counterstudies to liven up the scene, is a stunted imagination of the real. No one, perhaps, is born with that imagination full-blown, but history develops it out of its native elements. In the best readers it becomes virtually one of the senses. It is idle to argue that if the public (and historians and humanists as well) would similarly learn the "imagination of numbers," they would not be misled by "reports." As we just saw, the calculators themselves furnish in words the misinterpretation of their own numerical results. Talk and print everywhere conspire to make the percentage habit prevail at the expense of the concrete image. If "only 10 percent" of the young people exposed to fluorides in the water are likely to get pitted brown spots on their teeth (the assistant surgeon general's figure), the risk is negligible—because 1 in 10 in some other connection *is* negligible. Similarly, percentages and other measurements conceal the figures of actual count, closer to the historian's reality. When in 1963, Dr. Beeching in Great Britain launched his plan for cutting rail service by 1 percent of passenger miles and one-third of route miles, it was not evident that the reduction meant the elimination of 197,720,000 passenger miles and 9,384,330 individual journeys.* The

*For this difference in sensation between statistics and reality, Mr. Harry Hopkins, the author of a wide-ranging discussion of *The Numbers Game* (Boston, 1973), has coined the phrase "Statistical Diminution." The Beeching example and figures are from his work, p. 188.

point is not what action must be taken but what kind of judgment is generated by remoteness from the concrete. One often meets able persons in whom addiction to numbers has induced an impotence for passing any judgment without figures in support.

The need to estimate prevalence is of course frequent in writing history, the canon of generalization being: think first of negative instances. In the flush of gathering evidence and making discoveries, beginners are likely to herald their conclusions with "Never before . . ." and "He was unquestionably the first . . ." and "Throughout the period . . . ," none of which will stand up to the relevant negative instances. Public opinion could benefit from the same self-discipline. It is true that not all opposing facts are of equal weight or breadth, and some may be dismissed or taken as modifiers rather than destroyers of the large truth. That is where historical wisdom—indeed, tact—comes into play, and it obviously presupposes a well-stocked and well-practiced historical mind.

For what the practice of history does is to check the tendency toward hasty absolutes and to exercise the sense of alternatives. The march of mankind, being all opposition, contrast, divergent destiny, develops a taste for what is or could have been *other*. Thus Burckhardt meditates on Ignatius Loyola: "It is extraordinary that he did not found an order of penance, such as the Trappist order, but an entirely practical one, apparently with extreme intellectual effort, though directed by visions." Still more dramatically Burckhardt entertains a paradox: "The greatest boon for the Huguenot community was not the Edict of Nantes, but its revocation."

This turn of mind, negative in a creative way, indisposes toward belief in historical necessity. The errors of hindsight, which make past and present look inevitable, are prevented by the thought that the course of events (to quote Burckhardt again) "can never be determined by mere calculation. . . . One must . . . reckon with invisible forces, with miracles."[8] The last word is a figurative expression of the historian's familiarity with the inexplicable accident: "On the most inclusive expectation it could not have happened, but it did." The ideologies that flatter the love of order would not last as long as they do if historical minds were more numerous and more willing to go in for counter-propaganda. Everybody now scoffs at the theory of historical development and individual fate based on race. It seems absurd in the light of Russian, Chinese, Afro-American, Indian, and other achievements in domains once thought genetically reserved to Western white man. Yet it swayed the intellect of Europe for three generations. "Advanced" opinion trusted one or more of its elaborate formulas—Aryan, Nordic, Celtic, in addition to skull indexes and other "racial statistics." At any given time there is at least one such system in vogue, some grand scheme of causation and explanation or some lesser conspiracy theory for recent events. Against their absurdity not yet visible the only educative force is historical thought.*

An Antidote against Homogenizing

In ideology or conspiracy theories a prime need is to naturalize the disparate, to force discrepancies out of logic's way. Just as sociology makes of contemporary divorce a uniform event (which we know it is not), so retrospective psychiatry makes Henry VIII's motives for divorce uniform with modern motives, an assimila-

*A brilliant demonstration of historical thought riddling one of the lesser systems is Mr. John Sparrow's analysis of the conspiracy theories about President Kennedy's assassination and the Warren Report (*After the Assassination* [New York, 1967]). On a very different but functionally related subject, see *The Shakespeare Ciphers Examined* by W. F. and E. S. Friedman (Cambridge, 1957).

tion which only readers of history are likely to question. It takes both knowledge of facts and a sense of period to feel sure that Catherine of Aragon and the unfortunate Mrs. Jones upstairs are not parallel cases, and to remember that *royal* marriage and divorce and pre-Reformation religious belief are not immediately understood by likening them to ours—if indeed it is true that "we" share common conceptions of these matters across sectarian, social, and national barriers.*

To be sure, it is annoying to find or be told that what we took to be one is actually many. The mind loves unity, and now that even the chemical elements pass into each other, definitions and distinctions seem rigid and old-fashioned. The violent medleys of modern art favor blurring by analogy and prepare the eager intelligence to accept identities as soon as enunciated. Advanced sexologists, for example, tell their clients to regard their sexual concerns as they do matters of health. Some listeners object on moral grounds, but few on intellectual. It is evident that history and (even more

*Attempts at compromise between the historical view and the "fundamental" do not help. In the study by J. C. Flügel of Henry VIII's marriages, alluded to in the text, the very care taken by the writer to respect historical details shows up the weakness of the scheme. We hear about Henry's shrewd and detached political judgment, as well as about the unconscious drive, seesawing between the "egoistic and venerative," which controlled his amours and divorces. The drives are inferred from his early circumstances and later acts; they are in fact mere names summarizing those acts. But why other acts—say, of astute policy—remain outside the scope of the alternating drive is not explained. Nor is it clear why it is unconscious drive and not tradition that determined Henry's "desire for chastity in a sexual partner." Yet the final paragraph of the paper expresses no doubts: "Historical studies may well validate the psychoanalytic method and if the findings show psychoanalysis to be fundamentally true for all human beings, and not just the neurotic, then they will also show that the behavior of individuals long dead can be accounted for by the method *and perhaps in no other way*" (Italics added) (*International Journal of Psycho-Analysis* 1 [1920]: 55).

important) autobiography are not brought to bear on this piece of advice, which not only likens but *reduces* one thing to another, the difference in reality and the reality of difference being suppressed in a high-minded way. Persons who in theory reject such reductionism as a great error fall into it in practice, for lack of any defense more concrete than a philosophical warning. Cases must be cited, with enough detail to overcome abstract ideas. That is what Shaw did near the turn of the century when he successfully rid the "cultured classes" of the notion implanted by Max Nordau in a best-seller full of the psychopathology of the day, that all artists were mental degenerates. Shaw exclaimed: "What in the name of common sense is the value of a theory which identifies Ibsen, Wagner, Tolstoy, Ruskin, and Victor Hugo with the refuse of our prisons and lunatic asylums?"*

We know better than the nineties—or do we? Emotions, to our enlightened sight, are readily converted into their opposites or their forbidden extremes. What follows is that we are asked to read Mme de Sévigné's letters to her daughter as incestuous in feeling, after which it is a disappointment to hear that such an interpretation shows ignorance of history—the tone of the time and its accepted jokes on certain points.† Besides, history always insists that mixed motives are the rule, in flat oppposition to the itch for making the diverse identical and touting the product as "fundamental." When not long ago a man named Tuller and his

*Nordau's survey in *Degeneration* (1893) includes virtually every artist of the preceding half-century. Shaw's refutation, "The Sanity of Art," appeared in 1895. The quoted words are from the Standard Edition of Shaw's works (London, 1932), *Major Critical Essays*, p. 326.

†See the highly original study in which this correction is made, Philippe Ariès, *Centuries of Childhood* (New York, 1962), p. 105. The too present-minded interpreter was a recent editor of the Sévigné *Letters*.

sons tried to rob a bank, killed a policeman and a bank manager, then hijacked a jet plane to Cuba, the *New York Times* referred this erratic and criminal behavior to the older man's childhood under a cruel and hating father. That the man was also a declared enemy of "the system" and his raid undertaken in support of Castro was not mentioned. Later, after the family had corrected the "facts," the psychoanalytic story was partly retracted.[9] But political motive, conscious idea and purpose, have evidently become secondary if not superfluous in explaining action.

These examples, being interpreted, face the thinker with a choice: either belief in a fundamental drive that *undercuts* the mixture of motives, a fundamental cause that *governs* the mixture of events—or history. The issue is: the individual and his freedom. One would have thought that in our time of weary complaint against regimentation and standardization, when we are daily entreated by our sages to resist the overcrowding of the psyche with what is foursquare and nonhuman, no one could hesitate. Reading history would show it to be the realm of freedom, and not merely another borderland to be colonized by the mechanical. But apparently the urge to classify and abstract is stronger than the pain it inflicts, and history has to repel the attacks of those who could be its first beneficiaries.

An Antidote against Overintellection

And yet we should not be surprised. The pressures of machine civilization that cause the complaint also cause a turning away from words. The inarticulate arts are preferred (like the simultaneous use of several media) for their indistinctness of effect. Literature itself, in its advanced forms, has renounced the concrete and the consecutive. The novel, which for a century or more has thrived parasitically upon history, rejects narrative (no one wants a story) and decomposes character. It gives abstract notations of phenomena and creates new symbols for instinct.* Structuralism, as the movement is called which blends literature, anthropology, Marxism, and linguistics, is clear about its preference for the "underlying" and therefore universal.

But that same tendency is split at the root, for it periodically summons Western man to stop being "cerebral" and rediscover feeling, especially communal feeling.[10] Myth is deemed truer than logic (and than history, of course), though in this view it is not always clear whether myth is preferred for its fixed structure (intellect) or its adaptable poetry (emotion). The dilemma is in fact artificial. The either-or challenge to modern man is but a shove at the pendulum, which will swing back and smite the hand that shoved. Though the cognitive impulse may decline, it will not be "replaced"; the human mind enjoys it and life depends upon it. It is a mistake, besides, to regard science (abstraction, generality, system) as the only cognitive mode, or myth and poetry as the only modes of feeling. In the workings of the mind the separation of thought and feeling is but an abstraction for analytic purposes—though it may well be that in any one mind (including the public mind) thoughts and feelings are mismatched, to the owner's detriment.† It remains that thought, feeling, action are one; so much we know

*Nathalie Sarraute won fame with her novel *Tropismes,* the title of which denotes the kind of reflex found in organisms, say, exposed to light. When interviewed during the preparation of a later book she said: "In it I plunge deeper still into the kind of research that I haven't stopped pursuing since *Tropismes*" (quoted in Rayner Heppenstall, *The Fourfold Tradition* [New York, 1961], p. 270).

†At the conference of 1971 Professors Fritz Stern and Eugene Genovese both mentioned their practice of assigning students appropriate nineteenth-century novels to fill with concreteness and emotion the propositions of Marx, Nietzsche, and other social critics.

from the physio-psychologists of the last century, if not from self-observation.

Collingwood saw the importance of feeling for his contention that the past is actual here and now.[11] One does not need to accept his philosophy in order to admit that a reading of history reinforces by an immediate emotional experience the unseen effect of bygone events. The fit reader of a proper history is moved; he also thinks—or he would not be moved; and being changed by the experience, as Trevelyan noted, his actions are modified. The impossibility of tracing this sequence in detail does not make it doubtful; in matters of the spirit one is not following a barium meal through the intestines. When Pablo Neruda tells us that he read and reread the history of his native Chile for the heroism and poetry in the tragic civil war of three hundred years with the Araucanians, we can believe that his own work was fed by a mental re-enactment in which thought-feeling was continuous and indivisible.

When it is not a poet or a layman but a professional historian who undergoes such an experience, the form it takes may resemble this particular memory of work done on the Risorgimento: "I was zealous in turn for the House of Austria, the House of Savoy, the Papacy, the Mazzinian People, and half a dozen brands of liberalism or democracy."[12] These conflicting emotions in no way paralyze the will or reconcile the mind equally to all evils—on the contrary. The ill-assorted lumber that we all carry in our heads about nationhood, democracy, liberalism, the papacy, the Hapsburgs is rearranged and swept clean of cerebral dust. Coleridge speaks of "the calming power which all distinct images exert on the human soul."[13] The sort of calm produced by history's distinct images is a state in which thought and feeling are appropriate to their object and to each other.

That happy conjunction depends to a great extent on

the quality of the language in which the spectacle is re-created. An impoverished tongue cuts down full thoughts, and jargon vandalizes delicate feelings. Science and social science, we know, prefer technical abstraction.* Poetry tends to the colloquial, prose fiction is often a cipher, and the theater speaks in the lowest and most local ejaculations. It has not yet been found possible to write a history in any of these idioms. Through history speaking in common words and recognized syntax, a path can be beaten back to lifelike complexity and the subtlety of feeling-thought.†

It may be objected that the decline of vividness is chargeable as much to history as to the social sciences; for although history avoids technical words, it does not always avoid pedantry. This is true. Pedantry, once an eccentricity, is now a democratic right. Everybody may learnedly dither and quote at any length. Scholarship casts the great shadow of pseudo-scholarship on public print, much of which is formally "researched" and footnoted, while proliferating journals divide and subdivide their substance like amoebas, and articles are made out of the footnotes or glancing thoughts in the ripe scholarship of the 1890s. Readers, conditioned to masochism, fight shy of what is not sufficiently ponderous. It is the exception to find something pregnant

*It is curious to note that at the beginning of the nineteenth century a poet was already protesting against abstract answers to the questions he was asking about a friend's new occupation. Shelley writes to Peacock in 1819: "The devil take these general terms. . . . If it had not been the age of generalities, any one of these people would have told me what you did" (*Letters,* Aug. 22, 1819). The generalities, nascent in the Age of Reason, matured and multiplied in the Age of Revolution.

†It is the excess of dry phrasing and capsule thinking that makes the history textbook so hard to read and remember. The Duke of Saxe-Weimar is just "high-minded" and his policy in regard to Napoleon is nothing more than "favorable." There is no space to say more.

said in passing or to see it seized on when said. Thin texture and massive bulk go together in works that "blow" the mind (in Milton's sense) but do not feed it.*

It would be false to say that history in these days avoids thinness, pedantry, overbulk, and discouraging prose. But it is true that relatively to the rest of learned discourse, and experts' polemics apart, history has maintained clarity of expression quite as if the republic of letters still observed a common standard. The reason is not always superior judgment, but simple necessity: Events—the cab-and-truck collision at the corner—cannot be described without command of proper words in proper places. And the effect is to put the reader in touch once more with what is to be felt as well as understood.

An Antidote against Self-Centering

The thought that rhythmically recurs in reading history—"these were men . . . once alive . . . dead men, mistaken, once dead-sure . . . once held important . . . now footnote-fodder . . . once alive and hardly known . . . but now speaking to us . . . strange men . . . not strange to themselves . . . foolish, vicious, saintly, ordinary . . . like and unlike anyone we know . . . but once alive . . ."—the thought of men lost to time, in short, will in perceptive souls take care of every ego-urgency. In modern societies, with their short memories and strong opinion-making machines, some discourse is needed to suggest that the present scene will not always look the way it does now. A simmering down of excitement will occur, along with overturns of repute, discoveries of merit, and exposures of cheapness and lies where least expected. Whoever is appalled by the mere size of the enlarging anthill that

*See *Lycidas*.

happens to be his world need only glance at the pyramid of doings, artifacts, beliefs, passions, books, and great names in any quarter-century—say, from 1789 to 1815: it is now level dust, from which only certain actors, ideas, and events are still visible. A steady look at history checks the *hybris*—"we are the people"—that forever animates the contemporary. In history, contrary to common belief, the captains and the kings *depart*—all but a few; and with them, sometimes, the prophets and futurists. The latter's fallacies are especially vulnerable, like their presumption. For how can the future—the next ten years—belong to one who throws over the last ten, which incubated the evils and the plans he lives upon?

As for the unassuming opinion leader and the solid citizen, only reflection on history could show them that they, who now have doubts about machine civilization and the destruction of the environment, who incline toward equalizing conditions and abolishing error, are quite like the people who 150 years ago were for machine industry and the conquest of nature, and timidly hopeful of reducing the disparity of ranks by spreading education. Then and now they embodied similar motives, supported by the latest facts. Their zeal for progress would lift the burden of toil from mankind, their noble impatience would see freedom, peace, and knowledge prevail. The abstractions subsist, the contents flow in and out, ever new in tone and color. In the end, the "persistent issues" and "pressing problems" are not solved but abandoned. True novelty buries weary effort; boredom and surprise are also historical categories.*

*Toward the end of the fifteenth century, for example, the outlook in Europe was politically and morally gloomy: the Turk at the gate, violence and decaying institutions, church reform a failure: the Nuremberg Chronicle pictures general doom. But only a few years away were Columbus, Magellan, Luther, and Calvin with their revitalizing deeds and thoughts.

"Fusion" without "Re-tooling"

If history is "for the person," and his profit and pleasure come from a duly reconstructed past, then the vision and toil which produce a history must be the work of one man. This relation of writer to reader is essential to the effect: the single-minded view conveys the sensation one wishes to feel about one's own world. But history is interdisciplinary from the outset; its contents were mixed before the disciplines were invented. Therefore we lose its chief good if the crisscross feeling comes not from the events but from the attitudes of different narrators. And since attitudes often express methods, it follows that an effectual history —just like a course of instruction—must bear the impress of a single synthesizing mind.*

The fusion achieved by a competent historian-writer appears in his control over distracting multiplicity. But control means more than pattern-making and narrative arrangement. Long before he begins to write or even to study, the historian's power to seize on connections and to ask and answer questions bears his special mark. His work when done is valuable for individuality as well as for truth. Truth it must have, in intention and execution, but truth without character misrepresents the past and fails to grip the mind. The systematizers like to think they have a monopoly of "ordered knowledge," from which history is excluded. The fact of the matter is the other way around. It is the moral order of a history which enables us to say that Gibbon's history is a school of detachment and skepticism, Macaulay's a school of political virtue,[14] and Burckhardt's a school of esthetic sensibility. On the in-

*"No amount of uniform type and sound binding can metamorphose a series of individual essays into a book" (Woodrow Wilson on *The Cambridge Modern History*, in "The Variety and Unity of History," *Congress of Arts and Science*, etc. [Boston, 1906], 2: 14).

tellectual side, the fusion welds together uncommon talents and long training with imagination and sheer industry, e.g., Mommsen's legal mind, linguistic versatility, and tireless attention; Michelet's capacity for research, sense of drama, and genius for similitudes; Froude's heroic work in Spanish archives and judicious balance in describing character and policy. Whatever the powers, they must be obeyed. "Re-tooling" would be tempting Nemesis—or what are talents and inclinations for? Can one imagine Herodotus and Thucydides exchanging themes?

But is it possible, a reader may well ask, to receive from an ordinary history the same open and hidden benefits as those here attributed to the masterpieces? To which might be added the rider, Is it not better to read the newest, truest histories prepared by sober craftsmen not pretending to greatness, rather than mislead oneself with Carlyle's *French Revolution* and Michelet's Middle Ages? A very liberal-minded and imaginative theorist and practitioner, Professor G. R. Elton, has said that the great historians belong to prehistory and that the era of truth and virtue begins with Maitland and Namier.[15] The double doubt is sensible. No one is compelled to choose between the two kinds of history—if they are kinds. It was convenient here to make certain points by using historians whose names every reader would recognize. For each name cited, that of a living or recent historian could easily be substituted, though the choice might strike some as arbitrary. And scanning this later group, who is to say that the age of great historians has passed? Let us wait.

Meanwhile, the original question must be answered. In history as in every other activity of the spirit, the value of the communication depends on circumstance, intensity, predisposition. The choice of historical matter is enormous and the quality of "the historical" is found over a range that transcends the limited definitions here insisted on for didactic purposes. An essay such as G. M. Young's *Victorian England,* more topical than narrative and not on the grand scale, will afford nearly all the satisfactions of history, if one is equipped by earlier reading to understand its allusions. With the same proviso, a reader can be moved and enlightened by reading Norman Longmate's *King Cholera,* which is the history of that disease in nineteenth-century England.[16] He will learn many things (e.g., that Palmerston in old age was suspected of atheism for his public-health view of cholera), which other histories, whether of politics or religion, are not likely to bring out, but which illuminate the progress of secularism.

The maxim holds, then, that a reader of history *reads history,* just as a devotee of music goes to hear music, and a literary mind follows literature. They know nothing of the "Hundred Best Works" and want to know nothing of them under that rubric. For the student of history at his beginnings it is accordingly imperative that his appetite be hearty and catholic to the verge of indiscriminate. Just as abundant production is requisite for the happy occurrence of outstanding work, so abundant reading develops the original mind. It does so by forcing the student himself to frame a synthesis—his particular fusion—out of the diversity of other historical minds and the second sight of the events themselves. It is not the least of history's formative effects that its prime virtue of independence conspires with kindred independence in the beholder.

By Way of Conclusion: The Fair Sisterhood

The Limitations of History

Because the running reader's mind is impressionable, it may be that after thirty pages on the valuable effects of history the discipline will seem to have been put forward as a moral and intellectual panacea. Such an impression would be as unjustified as the belief that history was indeed all-sufficient. Collingwood's conclusion that historical thought is a unique and encompassing mode of grasping reality was rejected on an earlier page. But in this concluding chapter of summary and comparison it is useful to speculate about what prompted his assertion. Surely he was influenced by the feeling that much of contemporary culture had grown dry and thin: art deliberately skeletonized, religion turned into social work, philosophy preoccupied with language, literature *not* preoccupied with language, and the ologies fasting rather than feasting on mathematics.

Amid so much asceticism, history no doubt looks unfashionably plump and vivifying, but its powers have distinct limits. These limits were stated before as positive features: diversity, variability, uncertainty, and (in contrast with "depth") superficiality. This roster means that if history is health-giving it does not act automatically so, but only in the manner of physical exercise: it needs the will to use and enjoy it, coupled with the capacity to benefit, which is not a voluntary act. Only certain temperaments respond to history

—just as they gravitate toward certain religions and philosophies. On this very point William James divided thinkers into tough-minded and tender-minded. The tough in the present connection are the ones ready to stand uncertainty, and who therefore do not seek the guarantees of method and system. This affinity may seem to go against usage, which associates the rigor of system with the toughness of the scientist's uncompromising mind, but that is a misleading association. The "methodists" in history are gregarious and favor teamwork for the same reason that they consider plain history inadequate: it eludes the type of consensus provided by numbers; or, alternatively, provided by a universal structure—of the psyche, myth, or other absolute. History, rejecting absolutes, gives no comfort to the many able, subtle, dedicated minds that crave finality and certitude.

But what of Truth as an absolute goal, final and certain for all, even though only approximated by each? History does seek truth; it will not do to speak of history as if it were but another kind of art, for delectation and incidental wisdom. No intellectually honest historian forgets truth for an instant in the elaboration of his work. But—that is the triumph of history—truth absolute is not at hand; the original with which to match the copy does not exist. Accordingly, for the historian the word approximation conveys a false image; for if one professes to be nearing a goal, it must be known, or at least recognizable. The rationale of methods is precisely that they know the goal, having been previously tested by prediction and fulfillment. Thus they furnish at every step the guarantee of having the goal within the line of sight. Lacking method, the historian finds truth by the unremitting exercise of his and his peers' judgment upon the materials. Judgment is a comparative act that takes in the evidence and the report, and all evidences and reports together, and eliminates the untenable. The resulting truths are *built*, not reached, there being strictly nothing ahead to be reached. History is a bootstrap operation.

The "Methodists": Confidence without Independence

The tender-minded in search of fixity must consequently turn for satisfaction to special studies done according to method. We know that some theorists think the "new levels of understanding" not final; but perhaps the apparatus is reassuring enough to suggest that the levels are here to stay.* Whether or no, such studies have the intrinsic defect of being dependent on history, meaning, of course, on histories. Studies of types, institutions, and problems start from the same documents as history. More often still, they are tethered to one or two "standard" accounts of a period or leading figure. Usually, the psychoanalysts are better historians than the historians are psychoanalysts, which may only mean that history exerts a force not easily resisted. In any case, *as history*, the study can be no more solid than the ground it stands on; as psychology it stands or falls by the method and its management, which hardly need so indirect a test as an historical case.

One should not, of course, prejudge work not yet done by psycho-history and its siblings. Nothing said or implied in these pages has precluded the likelihood of useful studies being inspired and carried out by method. What has been categorically denied is that such studies would constitute either history or a new discipline fit to supersede history. To make the distinction clear, the theoretical claims denied may be recapitulated:

1. The pretended adjunctions and fusions are not

*See p. 63 above.

new, except in vocabulary (including that of mathematics).

2. The results are not history and neither are they science in the modern sense of the term, which implies measurement, prediction, and verification by repeatable experiment or observation.

3. The conclusions of typology and social analogy are not exact enough to guide public action, as the data of surveying, soil analysis, or other physical investigations are able to do.

4. Technical diagnosis or statistical analysis does not amplify understanding or finally explain persons and events, because it abstracts from their particularity in order to put in their place common denominators, mechanisms, averages, or trends.

What then may be the merits of special studies and what criteria should apply to them? The merits of the "new" studies are no different from those of the old and they are subject to the same standards. With or without scientific apparatus, special studies take up questions that are of small scope, or obscure, or moot, or time-consuming, or requiring uncommon knowledge to pursue. Among any of these belong numerical studies of what may be counted or sensibly estimated. William the Conqueror became their patron when he ordered the preparation of Domesday Book. "Uncommon knowledge" presides over the detailed discussion of such matters as the Wise Forgeries, the cause and circumstances of death in the "Black Hole of Calcutta," the psychological aspects of shipwreck, or the French Revolution's concern with public health.[1]

A more usual, but still special interest produces the analyses of battles and campaigns, social histories of epidemics, or such large undertakings as Captain (later Admiral) Mahan's systematic interpretation of modern history from the point of view of command of the sea. Very often the point of view *is* the contribution, the materials receiving little or no addition. Thus in his short and persuasive book on *Athenian Democracy* Professor A. H. M. Jones offers a remarkable distillation from the well-known sources, never before interrogated on this subject. Others have found out what Victorian readers read, how the French and English crowds behaved from 1730 to 1848, how everyday life was carried on in various times and places, how love was thought of and acted out in Greece and Rome, how professionalism and originality conflict in educational and cultural institutions, and why it is that the twentieth-century leisure classes have no leisure.[2] This last inquiry uses economics and several of the others make more or less use of non-historical methods.* To the random sampling one can add Freud's *Civilization and Its Discontents* (1930) without overstepping any clear-cut definition, for none exists. All the disciplines are sisters and can exchange gifts.

The virtue of a special study, descriptive or numerical, is that it furnishes the historian of an age or country the matter for a solidly based paragraph or page, or some incidental illustration or footnote. This ultimate use completes the cycle, since the author of the study relied (as we saw) on a previous history to discover his "question" or to quarry his substance. The conclusion is easy to draw: histories and special studies are preliminary to each other. There is no paradox in the relationship; it used to be expressed by the contrasted terms, history and monograph.†

It follows that the chief criterion of worth in special

*An interesting symposium on *Modern Methods in the History of Medicine*, ed. Edwin Clarke (London, 1971), brings out the importance of new techniques in paleopathology, as well as the use of the history of ideas in guarding against medical "facts" that have been recorded under the influence of untenable assumptions.

†"Originally, a treatise on a single genus, species, etc. of plant or animal" (*Webster's New World Dictionary of the American Language*, 2d ed. [Cleveland and New York, 1970]).

studies is utility. The prerequisites will be obvious to the reader who has followed the thesis of this book:

1. The special student's canons of evidence must equal the historian's in rigor.

2. The conclusion or diagnosis must be in the common tongue or translatable into it.*

3. Any comparative treatment of periods, events, or ideas must be warranted by a preponderance of concrete similarities and must not merely play with abstractions or imagery.†

4. Any system or method employed in obtaining the results must not be so embedded in them as to compel belief in both or none. Thus a history or biography may use the findings of a Marxist or Freudian study (and remain free of ideology as to causation) if in the study the elements of description and explanation are readily separable.§ Again, a history may incorporate figures elsewhere gathered and interpreted, but only insofar as it is clear in the study that the figures are not "constructed" and the interpretations do not edge over from the things actually counted to some other, more interesting situation.

*There is no use telling the reader of history that the great Dr. Thomas Beddoes, innovator, revolutionist, and medical attendant of Wordsworth and Coleridge, died of "compensatory emphysema of the right lung, contractive atelectasis of the left, and chronic purulent pericarditis," though this diagnosis is proper in the *Annals of Internal Medicine* (L. S. Gottlieb), 63 (September 1965): 532.

†For example, there is none of the historian's sanity in a comparison frequently heard in modern conversation, to the effect that the annual toll of death on the highways is a human sacrifice to the gods of the machine *just like* the sacrifices to the Minotaur or the gods of the Celtic druids.

§"With tact and skill he applies the insights of psychoanalysis to O'Neill's plays; about the man himself he provides us with the abundant detailed information he has collected . . . but leaves it to us to decide whether a fate like O'Neill's is finally shaped by the Freudian determinism" (Diana Trilling on Louis Sheaffer in *New York Times Book Review*, Nov. 25, 1973).

The Prospects of History

If, noticing the increased popularity of special studies and their new influence in making historians adopt the topical arrangement in place of the narrative,* one asks what the prospects are for history today, the answer must be given in two parts, one very tentative. The surer and briefer half of the prediction is that if a great history is written, it will be recognized and read. One meets not a few persons of education and experience, readers, but not of history, who catch fire on taking up by chance, say, Prescott's *Conquest of Mexico* or C. V. Wedgwood's two volumes *The King's Peace* and *The King's War* on the seventeenth-century revolution, or Mattingly's *The Armada.* The wide circulation of Barbara Tuchman's works also permits one to entertain the surmise just expressed, that the taste for history as a genre has not entirely died out, despite the vogue of biography, now turning more and more clinical and anti-heroic.

But great work ordinarily comes out of a milieu where similar talents abound: a great deal of painting or theology or writing must go on around the producer of the masterpiece. In historiography proper—though not in special studies—this concentration is nowhere apparent today as it was in the nineteenth century. Although history continues to nourish the mind of some as well as inspire the energies of others, both groups appear to be declining in numbers. Some of the most thoughtful—possibly the finest—spirits of the new generations are spurred by the visible decay of

*For example the latest volume in the Oxford History of Modern Europe is *France: 1848–1945*, by Mr. Theodore Zeldin. It is the first of a pair and is subtitled "Ambition, Love and Politics." The chapters are altogether topical: Notaries, The Rich, Children, The Genius in Politics, Bonapartism, etc. The work is in many ways admirable and engrossing, but it is not a history. Indeed, to get the best out of the book one should first find a good history series and read in it the volume entitled "France: 1848–1945."

present institutions to "find answers" to what ails us; they use history but do not cultivate it. They feel guilty when not at work on something of possible use immediately, and in one way or another they think that the mode of science is the only one that will yield serviceable results. This conviction behind their work they do not see as tantamount to unshouldering part of the burden of thought; nor do they see a contradiction between their humanitarian purpose and their counter-anthropomorphic methods. The implication of these remarks (still in the tentative mood) is not that these writers should abandon their aim to write history, but that they may lose their aim by abandoning the spirit of history.

That spirit has no agreed definition, but it might be epitomized by saying that its first principle is: Man has no nature. All the sciences and would-be sciences assert the contrary; to seize and dissect that nature is what they are in business for. Undoubtedly many historians would formally deny the epigram-postulate, yet it could be shown that they take it for granted in their work; for in facing their subject—dead people once alive—they are surprised by nothing, expect nothing, disallow nothing. They do not find it necessary to question physiology and ask whether organs and functions and the etiology of disease are sufficiently uniform the world over to give meaning to the idea of a single physical and instinctual nature of man. It is enough that in searching for what has happened by the agency of men everything and its opposite have equal likelihood and "reason." Awareness of this diversity does not run counter to any unities we perceive or promote—one human mind, one human race. These are indispensable axioms of modern civil society; but in concrete experience the practices, beliefs, cultures, and actions of mankind show up as incommensurable, even within one tradition. What else do we mean when we call "inhuman" the tribal exposing of unwanted children, cannibalism, and killing off the elderly, and when we impute "madness" to compulsory religious prostitution, dueling, slavery, or conquest for gain? A massacre must be a very human affair since it happens every day, and the horror and outcry are human too. If this unprejudging view of men is met by the argument that man's nature is "infinitely malleable," the conclusion is not altered. Malleability *is* non-nature; it commands nothing definite and predictable; the chameleon (figuratively speaking) has no *natural* color.

The last metaphor must not be misunderstood to mean that men are wholly fashioned from without. Their malleability is their freedom and they use it to "take" from the environment, from the past, from the alien whatever seems good to them. About these choices which help shape their culture, no prediction is possible either. All geographical and climatic "explanations" of cultures and their development have failed as badly as the racial explanation. The "same" produces unlike results and similar results arise from unlike conditions. Our old friend the Black Death *may* have led to superstition and religious remorse, but it also led to debauchery and vandalism.* Individuals and groups do

*Compare what is said about the aftermath of the plague in Agnola di Tura's *Cronica,* which with its continuation spans the years 1186 to 1352 ("the survivors did nothing but feast and seize and spend the belongings of those who had died without heirs": Muratori, *Rerum italicarum scriptores,* XV, col. 123) with Machiavelli's eloquent silence in the *Florentine History* (II, chap. 42), Boccaccio's description in the *Decameron,* and Burckhardt's judgment of later (bubonic) plagues in *The Civilization of the Renaissance in Italy,* Part VI, sec. 4. In 1973 nonetheless, a psychiatrist made prominent by his presidential connections felt entitled to write of "doctors who have conquered most of the plagues and *thereby* dispersed medieval superstitions" (italics added) (Arnold A. Hutschnecker, *New York Times,* November 20, 1973).

not all see the same realities, and from those they see they take hopes and fears that are not the same.

Anyone is free to reply that the *real* determinants are so numerous, and many of them so intangible, that we can never isolate them, yet "they are there." The enjoyment of that hypothesis is open to all, but its emptiness and remoteness unfit it for use in historical understanding. And to give up that understanding for a theoretical one which is by definition unattainable should seem to all those bent on immediate action for the good of man a circuitous kind of folly.

Man's multiform behavior as history delivers it brings us to the last point in our tentative survey of the prospects of history. The question for historians who have "fused" or are fusing with other disciplines is, Can they make the best of both genres for their own declared purposes?—the corollary question for the plain historian being, What does the public mind lose, if anything, in the migration to method?

The present-minded, it is clear, should insist on the malleability and multiformity of man, since they want to effect social change. They begin by "scientific" inquiry. But scientific method necessarily gives them a reading in no way suited to their needs. For what it ascertains is either unchanging fundamentals or contemporary "factors." The psyche has no history beyond one or two early accidents to its fixed structure. And the idea of a set of contemporary factors within a determinism being persuaded into better channels is as inconsistent as that of a gas engine developing traits of maturity and social ethics. The alternative to persuasion is coercion—what we do to raw materials ("nature") in order to make their mechanisms serve us. But coercion of human beings is what social philosophy purposes to abolish. It is a dead end.

For the plain historian the situation is at least not self-contradictory. He and his craft have survived attacks, bribery, neglect, invasion, and eclipse, perhaps because Clio is not a good mixer or of easy virtue. The greatest peril for her is the usurpation of her name and property, as James Harvey Robinson told an earlier generation apropos of theology: Saint Augustine let it influence his history-writing and then "induced that gloomy young man Orosius to compose a little treatise which, by reason of its strong appeal to a dominant conviction of succeeding ages, served to misdirect history . . . for a thousand years or more."[3*] These words contain a thought applicable to our condition. With profoundest respect for the performances of natural science, we must distinguish its productive spirit from the ways and signs to which its success has given authority. This contrast, it is not wrong to say, parallels that between a living faith and the theology giving technical form to belief. Theology has great uses, but like any other discipline it can decline into *mere* forms. The "theology of science" today attracts impatient minds who fear that their free thoughts, however solidly based, will not command assent, whereas they know that the forms of science compel belief. Having duly observed these "theological" forms, they feel quite plausibly that they stand within the circle of general acceptance. So strong is the "dominant conviction of the age."

Reinforcing it is the notion that the scientific is the most open and democratic mode of thought. Science admits of no art to conceal defects or cast favoring lights and shadows; it is a fair game at which any number can play after a common training in technique. As Pascal said, the rules, though couched in special terms, are simple. The honest user may not only count on attention to his findings, he will perhaps also control in their name some part of public action. What is eliminated by

**Seven Books against the Pagans* (ca. A.D. 415).

this "strong appeal to the dominant conviction" is the role of calculated common sense, which history, of all the humanities, is best able to sustain.

To see in the prospects of history a clue to the general condition of the Western mind is not to expect for history "misdirection for a thousand years." It is rather to connect in the normal historical manner several evidences that point the same way—the connection, for example, between the decline of individual freedom and the manipulatory implications of system, a "durable link" (one would say) that should concern the students of slavery. Indeed, the evidences point toward effects even more far-reaching. Method and system are capable of altering not merely social institutions but the mind itself. As Lionel Trilling pointed out in discussing the recent politics of literature, "If things are not singular, as once was believed and as the traditional novel urged us to believe, if a life is not to be seen as a history, then the end . . . is not decisive, things do not matter so much as they were thought to do, and the will need not put forth the effort that once was expected of it."[4]

A corresponding shift not surprisingly occurs in the objects of curiosity. It might be called a dehumanization, if as matter-of-fact historians we did not know that *all* human manifestations are human. A good illustration of this shift is the response (witnessed by the writer) of a group surrounding an eminent sociologist shortly after the recapture of Seoul from Communist occupation. It being the first event of the kind during the postwar struggles, an historian present envisioned and evoked the political and personal dramas, the polyglot armies, the leaders and populace—all the concomitants of an overturn in the equivalent of a war of religions. But the minds of the others were not really engaged until the sociologist broke in and said: "If one could get there now, what an opportunity to study the mechanism of attitude formation!"

Without the play of the historical sense upon public events and private memory, they are denatured, reduced to headline thoughts; they generate standardized fears and outcries—the fears that come with sudden darkness rather than those which spur resistance and the will to overcome adversity. Certainly, the long concentration on social history explained as the "movement" of "classes" has emptied the public mind of plain empirical realities. We end by not seeing what we have been told is not there to see. Hence the scorn for political history—and diplomatic and military. But why? The fates that spin have not forgotten them, and their formative effect might give strength to many when the foundations of the republic shake under the strokes of misgovernment and world crises.

The bloodless categories of classes and factors, forces and trends lack even the spare beauty of geometrical figures; they are indistinct and unimageable. Continuous debate about the refinement of "conceptual tools" leads moreover to marshaling evidence more and more minute, so as to be more exact. And by the same effort the cases seem less and less able to support the generalities, until the events themselves disappear: it is not only physics that has pulverized gross matter into particles *sans* properties.

In history this passion for the inorganic may be a good omen in that it cannot go much further. Analysis slices things finer and finer, taking heroic risks with the operator's fingers, but there comes a time when only the analyst is left and the scalpel might as well be thrown away. The work done during the last half-century on the culture of the modern ages since the Renaissance has been relentlessly analytic in all possible meanings of the word. Past and present surgical attempts on history have but conformed to a dominant habit. Their unquestioned acceptance as a modus operandi may mark the high point after which there is no other path but downward. If this is true, history may also be tumbled netherwards with all else and be for a time hidden from view. But it is not overconfident to prophesy that in any new vale which the muses may elect for their abode, Clio will again be found among them, *virgo intacta*.

NOTES

INTRODUCTION: WHO ARE THE DOCTORS?

1. *American Historical Review* 63 (January 1958): 284.

2. W. O. Aydelotte, A. G. Bogue, and R. W. Fogel, eds., *The Dimensions of Quantitative Research in History* (Princeton, 1972), p. 4.

3. "Historical Development and Present Character of the Science of History," *Congress of Arts and Science* (St. Louis, 1904), ed. Howard J. Rogers, 8 vols. (Boston & New York, 1905–7), 2: 111.

4. Langer, "The Next Assignment," pp. 284–85. See also *Psychoanalysis and History*, ed. Bruce Mazlish, 2d ed. (New York, 1971); and Robert Jay Lifton, "On Psychohistory," in *The State of American History*, ed. Herbert Bass (New York, 1970), pp. 276 ff.

5. "Luther's Early Development," *American Journal of Psychology* 24 (1913): 360–77.

6. See Harry Elmer Barnes, "Psychology and History," *American Journal of Psychology* 30 (1919): 337–76; and "Some Reflections on the Possible Service of Analytical Psychology to History," *Psychological Review* 8 (1921): 22–37; and John A. Garraty, "The Interrelations of Psychology and Biography," *Psychological Bulletin* 51 (1954): 569–82.

7. *Lee, the American* (Boston, 1912), pp. 269 ff., and *New York Post Literary Review* 3 (1923): 641–42.

8. See the Foreword to the *Comédie humaine* (1843).

1. THE QUESTION OF SUBSTANCE

1. *Judgments on History and Historians*, trans. Harry Zohn (Boston, 1958), p. 241.

2. Langer, "Next Assignment," pp. 292–302.

3. Christopher Lehmann-Haupt, *New York Times*, May 11, 1972.

4. Weinstein and O. G. Lyerly, in *Psychiatry* 32 (February 1969): 1.

5. "Essay on Materials and Method," *Slavery* (Chicago; 1959, 2d ed., 1968), p. 224.

6. Eugene D. Genovese, *The World the Slaveholders Made* (New York, 1969), p. vii.

7. Ibid., Part II, chap. 2.

8. Ibid., pp. 149, 150.

9. David S. Landes and Charles Tilly, eds., *History as Social Science* (Englewood Cliffs, N.J., 1971), pp. 46–47.

10. Ibid., p. 12.

11. Review of *The History Primer,* by J. H. Hexter, *Encounter* 40 (April 1973): 64.

12. Ibid.

2. THE QUESTION OF METHOD

1. Elkins, *Slavery,* pp. 115–23.

2. *Civilization and Its Discontents,* trans. Joan Riviere (Anchor Books, 1958), chap. 8, pp. 103–4.

3. By Robert S. Woodworth and Mary R. Sheehan, 3d ed. (New York, 1964).

4. Franz From, *Perception of Other People,* with a Foreword by Henry A. Murray (New York, 1971).

5. Ibid., pp. 148–49.

6. William J. McGill, "Neural Counting Mechanisms and Energy Detection in Audition," *Journal of Mathematical Psychology* 3 (1967): 369–70.

7. Cf. the reviews of: N. G. Clinch, *The Kennedy Neurosis* (1973), R. J. Lifton, *Home from the War* (1973), W. C. Langer, *The Mind of Adolf Hitler* (1972), and E. Tangye Lean, *The Napoleonists* (London, 1970); as well as G. R. Elton's skepticism about the value of Erikson's *Young Man Luther* (*The Practice of History* [New York, 1967], p. 25 n.).

3. THE QUESTION OF EVIDENCE

1. F. W. Bateson, *Wordsworth, a Re-interpretation* (London, 1954; 2d ed., 1956).

2. Walter C. Langer, *The Mind of Adolf Hitler* (New York, 1972), p. 151. The italics were used by Professor Hans W. Gatzke in his review of the work (*American Historical Revew* 78 [April 1973]: 398), to which the comments in this book are much indebted.

3. *Slavery,* pp. 224–26.

4. *Henry James: The Master* (New York, 1972), pp. 294–301. William James's letter is in the archives of the National Institute of Arts and Letters (New York); it was printed in the *New York Times Book Review* for April 16, 1972, and *The* (London) *Times Literary Supplement* for September 15, 1972.

5. Freud, *The Psychopathology of Everyday Life,* trans. and ed. A. A. Brill (London, 1956), p. 183. (In the Standard Edition of Freud's works, ed. James Strachey, 6:227.)

6. Ibid., p. 184. (Standard Edition, 6:229.)

7. Edward Marjoribanks, *Edward Marshall Hall* (London, 1929), p. 203.

8. Sir Sydney Smith, *Mostly Murder* (London, 1959), p. 260.

9. Freud, *Psychopathology of Everday Life,* Brill ed., p. 132. (Standard Edition, 6:169–70.)

10. *Daedalus* 97:695.

11. *New York Times Book Review,* Dec. 20, 1970.

12. Erikson, *Daedalus* 97:695.

4. THE QUESTION OF MOTIVE

1. William J. McGill, "Neural Counting Mechanisms and Energy Detection in Audition," *Journal of Mathematical Psychology* 3 (1967): 351, 361.

2. Landes and Tilly, eds., *History as Social Science,* pp. 45–47.

3. Philip Marsden, *In Peril before Parliament* (New York, 1965), pp. 64–65.

4. *Rutherford B. Hayes and His America* (New York, 1954), pp. 74, 81.

5. See *The Myth of Mental Illness* (New York, 1961) and *The Ethics of Psychoanalysis* (New York, 1965).

6. *Essays in Fabian Socialism* (London, 1889), p. 191.

7. "The Study of History," *Cornhill Magazine* 4 (1861):32.

8. *Correspondance,* ed. Georges Roth (Paris, 1957), 3:275.

9. Christopher Lehmann-Haupt, *New York Times,* Aug. 6, 1973.

10. "On Psychohistory," in *The State of American History,* ed. Herbert Bass (New York, 1970), p. 295.

11. *New York Times,* Nov. 1, 1973.

5. HISTORY AS COUNTER-METHOD AND ANTI-ABSTRACTION

1. Freeman: Introduction to Mommsen's *History of Rome,* trans. W. P. Dickson (Everyman ed., 1:xiii); Woodrow Wilson, "The Variety and Unity of History," *Congress of Arts and Science,* etc. (Boston, 1906), 2:15.

2. *Epistolae* 5, 8, 4.

3. *Medieval Church and Society* (New York, 1972), p. 47.

4. *The Psychopathology of Everyday Life,* trans. and ed. A. A. Brill (London, 1956), p. 80. (Standard Edition, 6:101).

5. Charles C. Fries, *American English Grammar,* National Council of Teachers of English (New York, 1940).

6. Edited by David S. Landes and Charles Tilly (Englewood Cliffs, N.J., 1971), pp. 45–46.

7. G. J. Renier, *History: Its Purpose and Method* (Boston, 1950), p. 49.

8. G. O. Trevelyan, *Life and Letters of Macaulay* (any edition), Macaulay's diary under dates: Dec. 18, 1838, Nov. 5, 1841–July 1843, Dec. 10, 1845, July 17, 1848.

9. Landes and Tilly, p. 20.

10. "The Variety and Unity of History" (see note 1 above), pp. 15, 17.

11. Bernard DeVoto in *Biography as an Art,* ed. James Clifford (London, 1962), pp. 144–50.

12. Plumb, *The Death of the Past* (Boston, 1970), p. 138.

6. THE FORMATIVE EFFECT OF HISTORY

1. *Guy Mannering,* chap. 37.

2. The first dictum about history repeating has become a proverb, though found more formally stated in antiquity, for example in Plutarch ("Sertorius"). Sir Walter Raleigh makes a point of the advantage of precedent in his *History of the World.* The second commonplace is implied in all the statements about the falseness and futility of history. The third is in Hegel's (*Philosophy of History,* Introd.) amplified by Aldous Huxley; and the last is in Santayana's *Reason in Common Sense* (p. 284), paralleled by Ortega y Gasset in *The Revolt of the Masses* and elsewhere.

3. *Medieval France* (Oxford, 1929), p. 130.

4. *Clio, a Muse and Other Essays* (London, 1913), pp. 20–21.

5. *The Will to Power* (1888), sec. 974.

6. See the *Bulletin of the Council for Basic Education* (Washington), June and September 1967, pp. 8–10 and 12–14.

7. *New York Times*, Nov. 18, 1973.

8. *Judgments on History and Historians* (Boston, 1958), pp. 136, 149.

9. Abraham Kalish, "Report on Accuracy in Media," *The Rising Tide*, Jan. 15, 1973, p. 7; and *New York Times*, Oct. 30, 31, Nov. 1, 6, 1972.

10. Theodore Roszak, *The Making of a Counterculture* (New York, 1969), pp. 50–51.

11. See Louis O. Mink, *Mind, History, and Dialectic* (Bloomington, Ind., 1969), p. 158.

12. Sir Keith Hancock, *Country and Calling* (London, 1954), p. 220.

13. Lecture XIII of his 1818 series. See *Lectures on Shakespeare, Etc.* (Everyman ed.), p. 312.

14. Herbert Paul, "Macaulay and His Critics," *Anglo-Saxon Review* 4 (March 1900): 124.

15. *The Practice of History* (New York, 1967), p. 4.

16. London, 1966.

BY WAY OF CONCLUSION: THE FAIR SISTERHOOD

1. In order of citation: John Carter and Graham Pollard, *An Enquiry into the Nature of Certain Nineteenth-Century Pamphlets* (London, 1934); Macdonald Critchley, *The Black Hole and Other Essays* (London, 1964) (contains the study of shipwreck); Dora B. Weiner, "Le Droit de l'homme à la santé," *Clio medica* 5:209 ff.

2. In the order listed: A. H. M. Jones, *Athenian Democracy* (Oxford, 1964); A. B. Cruse, *The Victorians and Their Books* (London, 1962); G. Rudé, *The Crowd in History, 1730–1848* (New York, 1964); W. M. Flinders Petrie, *Social Life in Ancient Egypt* (London, 1923); Pierre Grimal, *L'amour à Rome* (Paris, 1967); F. H. Hayward, *Professionalism and Originality* (London, 1917); Staffan B. Linder, *The Harried Leisure Class* (New York, 1970).

3. "The Conception and Methods of History," *Congress of Arts and Science, St. Louis, 1904* (Boston, 1906), 2:41.

4. "Art, Will, and Necessity," unpublished lecture, autumn 1973, Ms. p. 18.

CHECKLIST OF WRITINGS ON HISTORIOGRAPHY BY JACQUES BARZUN

(Prepared by Virginia Xanthos Faggi)

1. Review of *The Jacobins,* by C. Crane Brinton. *The Historical Outlook,* January 1932.
2. Review of *Does History Repeat Itself?* by R. F. McWilliams. *The Historical Outlook,* February 1933.
3. Review of *The Pendulum of Progress,* by Sir George Young. *The Historical Outlook,* February 1933.
4. "The Uses of History"; review of *Historian and Scientist,* by Gaetano Salvemini. *Saturday Review of Literature,* December 23, 1939.
5. "Truth in Biography: Leonardo and Freud." *University Review* (Kansas City), June 1940.
6. Review of *Nietzsche* by Crane Brinton. *Saturday Review of Literature,* March 22, 1941.
7. "Romantic Historiography as a Political Force in France." *Journal of the History of Ideas,* June 1941.
8. "Using the Past"; review of *The Ground We Stand On,* by John Dos Passos. *Nation,* September 13, 1941.
9. "Our Tradition and Its Critics"; review of *From Luther to Hitler,* by William M. McGovern, and *What Nietzsche Means,* by George Allen Morgan. *Saturday Review of Literature,* September 27, 1941.
10. "Max Eastman and History." *New Leader,* February 14, 1942.
11. "Finding Parallels and Finding Scapegoats." WABC broadcast "Living History," May 12, 1942.
12. "Recent European Historians"; review of *Some Historians of Modern Europe,* edited by Bernadotte E. Schmitt. *Nation,* April 4, 1942.
13. "The Bridge of Clio"; review of *A History of Historical Writing,* by James Westfall Thompson. *New Republic,* December 7, 1942.
14. "History, Popular and Unpopular"; chapter in *The Interpretation of History,* edited by Joseph R. Strayer. Princeton, 1943.

15. "Men and History"; review of *The Hero in History,* by Sidney Hook. *Nation,* September 18, 1943.

16. (With others) *Introduction to Naval History.* New York, 1944.

17. "The Muse Resents the Soapbox"; review of *Man the Measure,* by Erich Kahler. *Saturday Review,* May 13, 1944.

18. Review of *The Philosophy of American History,* by Morris Zucker. *Saturday Review,* March 31, 1945.

19. "History as a Liberal Art." *Journal of the History of Ideas,* January 1945.

20. "Cultural History: A Synthesis"; chapter in *The Varieties of History,* edited by Fritz Stern. New York, 1956.

21. Review of *The Nature of Biography,* by John A. Garraty. *Mississippi Valley Historical Review,* March 1958.

22. "The Scholar-Critic"; chapter in *Contemporary Literary Scholarship,* edited by Lewis Leary. New York, 1958.

23. (With others) *The Education of Historians in the United States* (written by the Committee on Graduate Education of the American Historical Association). New York, 1962.

24. "Truth in Biography: Berlioz"; chapter in *Biography as an Art,* edited by James Clifford. London, 1962 (reprinted with revisions from *The University Review* [Kansas City], 1939).

25. "Exploring the Space of Time"; review of *The Treasures of Time,* by Leo Deuel. *Mid-Century* (New York), no. 42, Summer 1962.

26. "The Spectre of Decadence"; review of *The Decline of the West,* by O. Spengler. *Mid-Century,* no. 43, August 1962.

27. *Race: A Study in Superstition.* Rev. ed. (chapters 2, 4, 8–11). New York, 1965.

28. "Ideas Just in Time"; chapter in *Naturalism and Historical Understanding,* edited by John P. Anton. Albany, 1967.

29. "Bagehot as Historian." Introduction to *The Historical Essays of Walter Bagehot.* Collected Works, vol. 3. London, 1968 (Harvard University Press, 1970).

30. (With Henry F. Graff) *The Modern Researcher.* Rev. ed. New York, 1970.

31. "Psychology and History"; speech at the Conference on Psychology and History sponsored by the Graduate Center of the City University of New York, April 24, 1971; not published; transcript of conference tape.

32. Review of *Sources of Cultural Estrangement,* by Deric Regin. *Canadian Journal of History,* September 1971.

33. "History for Pleasure: A Self-Justifying Sport"; speech in the National Humanities Series for the New Canaan Historical Society, October 18, 1971; not published; transcript of tape.

34. "History: The Muse and Her Doctors." *American Historical Review,* February 1972.

35. "Thomas Beddoes or, Medicine and Social Conscience." *Journal of the American Medical Association,* April 3, 1972.

36. "The Mystery in Rameau's Nephew"; review of *Diderot the Satirist,* by Donald O'Gorman. *Diderot Studies XVII,* 1973.

37. "The Point and Pleasure of Reading History." *Encyclopaedia Britannica.* Vol. 1. New Edition. Chicago, 1974.

INDEX

(Prepared by Virginia Xanthos Faggi)